# MEAT
## AND GAME COOKBOOK

# Contents

# About this Book

The new *Good Cook's Library, Meat and Game Cookbook*, with its unusual variety of recipes will excite everyone who eats meat and who cares about its quality. This carefully put together book is a treasure trove of delicious, famous, inexpensive, festive, and easy-to-make meat dishes.

The recipes, all specially photographed for this cookbook, will entice one to try them out after leafing through the book for the first time. Every recipe is explained so simply that even novice cooks will be able to make them. Roasting, braising, grilling, and broiling are made fun and easy. The notes on preparation and cooking time allow for sensible planning of any menu. Also included are comments indicating whether a dish is more or less expensive, whether it is easy or difficult to make, and whether or not it is a famous recipe or regional specialty.

Be sure to read through "The Value of Meat." Listed here are healthy reasons to include meat in one's diet. The differences between the various types of meat, beef, veal, pork, lamb, and game are considered.

The recipes are divided into four chapters. The first is "Sauteed Dishes," all of them quick meals. These are particularly important for households in which there is little time for preparing meals. Schnitzel, cutlets, steaks and kebabs, are all included and are best served with fresh salads or young vegetables. "Fine Braised Dishes" in the next chapter are valued by connoisseurs. Among these are tender fricassees, refined ragouts, creations with chopped meat, and hearty chunks from the stew pot. Next are "Festive Roasts," which could not have been left out of this book—above all in the case of roast beef, Beef Wellington, Chateaubriand, calf kidneys and rabbit with juniper cream. The last chapter offers "Chilled Delicacies." Here there are cold roast meats with attractive accompaniments, steak tartare with quail eggs, terrines, and vol-au-vents. They are all appropriate for a cold buffet, but also for supper or a special picnic.

In order to learn the proper handling of meat in one's own kitchen, there is a section with step-by-step photographs showing what to watch for when breading meat, how to cut a pocket, how to create a cordon bleu, and how to make roulades keep their shape. In addition, explained step-by-step are techniques on how to prepare roast beef or rolled roast, how to place a net around a pork roast, and how to lard meat. Demonstrated are typical ways to cook steaks to varying degrees of doneness, and how to prepare tender innards. To present roasts beautifully, study the short course in carving, again with step-by-step photographs. A complete roasting table helps determine roasting times for various cuts of meat.

Get carried away by this book's bright pictures, by a fine piece of meat from the butcher, by the family's taste and that of friends, and by one's own whims. Discover a recipe for all the favorite meat dishes.

Have fun trying out these recipes! Bon appetit.

# The Value of Meat

### The Value of Meat
Meat is not only an important means of nourishment, but also a much appreciated one. Many inhabitants of industrialized countries cannot even imagine a meal without meat.

### The Pros and Cons
The health value of meat is defined: meat provides protein, which is indispensible for the maintenance of life. The protein of meat is of biologically high quality and the body readily absorbs iron from meat. Meat has a high saturation value and also provides varying quantities, according to the type of meat, of minerals and vitamins. In recent years one has heard and read much concerning the disadvantages of meat, as well as concerns about cholesterol. And then there is a general condemnation of veal, because of harmful feeding methods. Yet, meat still remains a primary source of protein.

The U.S. Government has established grade protection by labeling all meat sold through interstate commerce. The U.S. grading scale is based on six classes: prime, well-flavored, fine textured, tender meat which contains white fat; choice, high quality meat, tender and juicy with less fat; good, relatively tender with a higher ratio of lean portions to fat; standard, usually has a bland flavor; commercial and utility, a poor grade which is tough with a coarse texture.

### Beef
Beef is distinguished according to the type of animal it comes from, whether a bull, a heifer, a cow, an ox or a calf. Higher quality meat comes from heifers, young oxen, or from cattle raised for their meat. Young bulls can also give good meat. For quick roasting, the best meat has short fibers, is marbled with fat, and has a dark red color. The commercial cuts of beef include: round, which yields rump and round steak; sirloin; short loin, which includes the T-bone cut; rib; chuck, which yields pot roast; foreshank, which yields brisket; short end of brisket; and flank.

### Veal
Up to the age of 3 months, young male or female cattle are called calves. Calf meat—veal—is pink or yellowish-pink, is lean and easy to digest. The commercial cuts of veal include: shank, shoulder, rib, loin, leg, breast, and flank.

### Pork
Compared with beef, pork has less and softer connective tissue. Therefore, it is a high quality meat. This meat is usually designated "tender and juicy." It is fresh when red and lightly streaked with fat. Bacon should be clear and firm.

### Lamb
Lamb is the generic name for both lamb and mutton. The meat of milk lambs is light pink, that of feed lambs the color of smoked salmon. Lamb fat is white. The meat of mutton is a dark brick red, the fat yellowish. The commercial cuts of lamb include: leg; loin, which yields loin chops; rack of rib; breast; neck; shoulder; and shank.

### Storing Meat Properly
Fresh meat should be stored at 42 degrees. Beef should be kept loosely wrapped, and if enveloped in fat, it can be left uncovered. A general rule of thumb: the larger the cut of meat, the longer it can be safely stored. Veal, lamb and pork are more perishable than beef and should not be kept in the refrigerator for lengthy periods of time.

Uncooked meat that is cubed or diced should be used within 48 hours. Ground meat and sausage are the most perishable meats and should be used within 24 hours.

# Preparing Meat

## Breading Meat

Crisp breading of flour, eggs and crumbs insures that tender pieces of meat will stay juicy. A breading can be made finer by adding grated cheese to crumbs or spices to flour. Dry the meat well, to make sure that the breading will stick to it. Rub salt into the meat and dredge in flour right away.

Dip both sides of the meat into a batter of egg and water. The water makes the breading more resilient.

## A Pocket for Stuffing

Stuffing lends meat more flavor and increases the portions. Any ingredient that would not overwhelm the meat is suitable, like cheese, ham, herbs, eggs, crumbs, or soft bread.

Do not cut pockets into long, thin pieces of meat, rather, put the filling over half of one side and fold the other half over to make the pocket. Fasten with toothpicks.

## Cordon Bleu

The combination of a savory filling and a crisp breading requires an especially delicate preparation. Cordon bleu is filled with thin slices of cooked ham and Swiss cheese. The size of the pocket depends on the size of the piece of meat.

Pat dry two thin veal schnitzel, spice to taste, and place 1 slice of ham and 1 slice of cheese on each. If desired, a pickle can also be added..

## Roulades

One favorite method of varying meat dishes is to fill, roll, and stew thin slices of meat. Scallopini or cutlets are best for veal or pork, while cuts from a tip roast are best for beef. The slices of meat should be long, thin, and have squared corners. The stuffing is really up to the imagination, but it should always contain some fat.

Lay or spread the stuffing onto the strips of meat, leaving the edges free.

Dredge the meat in the crumbs and shake off any excess breading. Crumbs in the cooking oil burn quickly.

Roll the back of a large knife over the breading for a latticed effect. This keeps the breading from tearing open while cooking.

Take a sharp knife and cut the deepest possible pocket into a thicker slice of meat, but do not separate the two sides.

Loosely fill the pocket with the stuffing. Either pin the pocket with toothpicks or sew it shut with kitchen string.

Lay the second schnitzel over the first and pin the two together using tooth-picks.

Dredge the stuffed schnitzel first in flour, then egg, and finally in bread crumbs.

Depending on the stuffing, fold in the sides to avoid losing any of the filling when the meat is rolled.

Use skewers, roulade pins, or cooking yarn to hold the rolls together. Do not use plastic string. Remove yarn, pins, or skewers before serving.

# Preparing Meat

## Roast Beef

Roast beef is one of the finest cuts of beef and should be treated accordingly. A larger roast of about 2 pounds usually works best. One should always rinse the meat under cold water and carefully pat dry.

Use a thin, sharp knife to remove any membrane or other tough material.

## Meat in a Pork Net

Schweinenetz is a familiar part of French cuisine. Farces are wrapped in it and broiled as ennobled rissoles. The net holds the meat together, for example, when a roast is prepared with mustard or some other spreadable. One could even wrap a Beef Wellington in the pork net instead of the dough. It bastes the roast during cooking, while protecting it from drying out. Be sure to check with the butcher or grocer's meat department to be sure that they have it.

Rinse and dry the rump roast, then brown it on all sides in very hot fat to seal all the pores. Let the meat cool or spread on a stuffing.

## Rolled Roast

A flat piece of meat like a breast of veal or shoulder of lamb works best, but be sure there are no bones. The meat can be rolled with a filling or simply spiced.

Remove all membranes, tendons, and excess fat with a sharp knife. Cut so that the meat is evenly flat, reserving any trimmings for a farce or sauce.

## Stuffing a Roast

Large roasts can be enhanced in taste and visual attractiveness by stuffing. Never fill it completely, otherwise the pocket may break open. If some stuffing is left over, then bake it in a small pan next to the roast and serve as a side dish.

Make a pocket by separating the connecting tissue between the two main layers of meat.

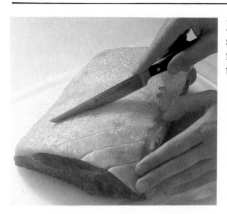

Make lattice shaped incisions on the fat side of the roast, but do not cut into the underlying meat.

Rub salt and pepper into the meat, then brown in fat on all sides to seal in the juices. Place in the oven with the fatty side up and cook to the desired degree of doneness.

Rinse the pork net well and dry carefully between towels.

Spread out the pork net, place the meat in the middle, and wrap it completely in the net, then cook according to the recipe.

Rub spices into one side, or spread a filling on it, then roll.

Tie up the roll with kitchen string, not plastic string, as if it were a package, wrapping the string around the roll every 2 inches.

First brush or rub the recommended spices into the pocket, then loosely fill in the stuffing.

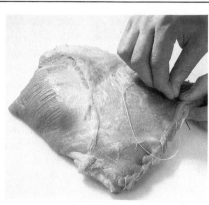

Fold the ends of the pocket over one another. Sew the edges together with kitchen string and tie off the ends. Do not use plastic string.

# Preparing Meat

## Barding Venison

Game is very lean and must be protected from drying out by the addition of fat. This does not damage the tender muscle tissue. The strips of bacon or fat are removed shortly before the roast is done to allow it to brown.

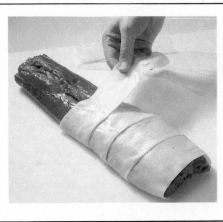

Thinly slice firm fresh fat, making the slices big or small enough for the roast. Cover the meat with fat, leaving no gaps.

## Latticed Barding

Lean and tender veal roasts could also use a little extra fat while roasting, especially since it can take some time. Veal is difficult to digest if not thoroughly cooked. For barding, use thin strips of fresh pork fat.

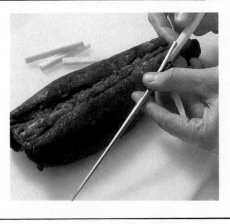

Cut the fat into ½ to 1-inch wide strips, which should be as long as possible (this makes weaving the lattice easier).

## Larding the Surface

This is another way to get excellent results with lean meat. It does take a little more work than barding, though. It is important to put the strips of fat into the freezer before larding to make them less likely to tear.

Take the ¼-inch thick strips of fat and fasten them to the end of a larding needle.

## Penetrating Larding

This method is appropriate for lean cuts of beef that are roasted. The meat gets the fat it needs from inside. Whatever fat comes out of the meat goes into the juices and can be spooned off. The remaining strips of fat add flavor to the meat and make an attractive pattern when the meat is carved.

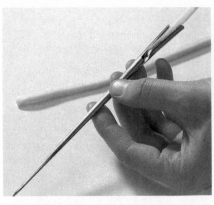

Pull long, chilled strips of fat through the meat with a penetrating larding needle; the needle has a V-shaped or round "gutter".

Secure the strips of fat or bacon with kitchen string and knot the ends of the string.

Baste the roast regularly while cooking. After removing the fat, raise the temperature to brown the meat quickly.

First do one row of strips, then weave in the crossing strips, once over, once under the first strips.

Tie the roast with kitchen string to keep the fat from falling off. Do not use plastic string.

Make 1-inch holes under the surface of the meat with the larding needle and pull the strips of fat into them.

Let the ends of the fat strips stick out about 1 inch on either end.

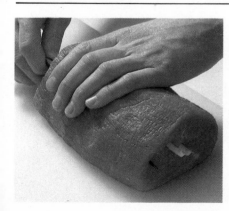

Penetrate the meat in evenly-spaced places, following the grain and pulling the strips of fat into the meat.

Allow the strips of fat to stick out at either end. Rub the recommended spices into the meat before cooking.

# Carving Meat

## Large Boneless Roasts

The rule of thumb is to cut meat across the grain. Finely grained meat, like roast beef, should be cut in very thin slices (about ¼ inch thick), while coarser-grained meat should be cut into ½- to 1-inch thick slices. If a roast appears to be too large for one meal, then only half should be carved, in order to keep the larger piece warm longer and to keep the meat from drying out if it needs to be stored. Hard crusts or other pieces of meat that would be difficult to carve are cut off before slicing the meat and apportioned to whoever wants these parts.

The best surface for carving meat is, of course, a large carving board with grooves for the juices. Rinse it with cold water to keep the wood from absorbing the juices. Juices that run out of the meat when carving will be trapped in the grooves. If one of these carving boards is not available, then use the serving platter as the base.

## Legs and Rib Roasts

Carving roasts with bones depends on the bone. With a rib roast, one should have the butcher prepare the meat so that it will be easy to carve later. For a leg, there are two methods of carving one can use, depending on size and shape of the cut.

For smaller legs, slice the meat diagonally from the bone. Leave the carvings leaning against the bone or arrange them on a platter.

## Tenderloin Roasts

Venison and rabbit roasts are most often carved according to these suggestions. For festive occasions, however, one might also serve lamb, veal, or piglet roasts. Important: Always let a roast sit in the turned off oven for a few minutes, the larger the roast, the longer it should sit. This way, the juices in the roast will be evenly distributed throughout the meat and one will not lose so much during carving.

Lay a venison back on the carving board and cut through the back all the way to the backbone.

## Large Steaks

Steaks that weigh up to two-thirds of a pound are considered one portion and are served intact. Large steaks, however, like London broil, porterhouse, or T-bone can weigh between 1 and 2 pounds and could represent 2 to 4 portions. These must be carved before serving. Important: Steaks must be carved quickly to avoid heat loss. The portions are arranged on hot plates and served right away.

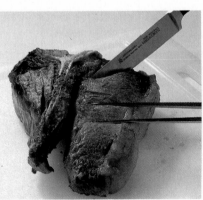

Steaks with bones should be held in place with the back of the carving fork while being boned. The bone of a porterhouse steak is less pointed than that of a T-bone steak.

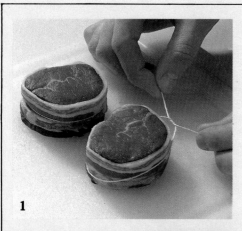
1

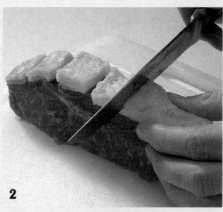
2

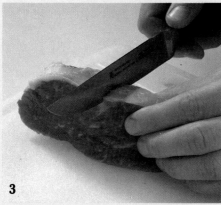
3

4

# Steaks

These expensive cuts of meat should be aged before cooking. Careful preparation is necessary to insure attractive shapes and even cooking.

**1** Tournedos are made from the end of the fillet. They should not be flattened, but bound horizontally with kitchen string. Also a strip of fat may be wrapped under the string and removed before serving.

**2** Rump steak is cut from the longer flat roast beef and has a fatty rind on one side. This should be cut in 1 inch intervals and takes a typically comb-like shape during cooking.

**3** Entrecote, the large steak made from a flat roast, has a large tendon in the upper layer of meat. This must be severed to keep the meat from curling during cooking.

**4** A porterhouse steak can weigh up to 2 pounds and be about 2½ inches thick. Cut away the meat next to the bone before cooking so that it will cook as fast as the other parts.

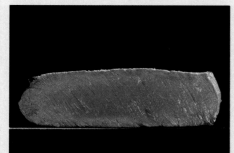
1

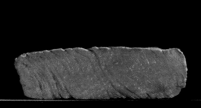
2

3

4

# Degrees of Doneness

With steaks, it is not just the quality of the meat that determines the flavor, the cooking time plays an important role as well. Connoisseurs order their favorites according to the following standards.

**1** Very rare: The steak is brown in only a thin layer on either side, inside it is still bloody and raw. It is very tender to the touch.

**2** Rare: The steak is brown on the outside, pink further in, and still red in the very middle. Only the middle part should be very tender to the touch.

**3** Medium: The meat is pink inside and firm to the touch.

**4** Well done: The steak is crispy brown outside, fully cooked, and firm.

# Recommended Cooking Times

1) The roaster should be large enough to allow 1 to 2 inches of space all around the meat. Large roasts should be started with the fat side down, then turned around after half of the cooking time has passed.

2) A roast can become tender only if it is moistened constantly while being cooked. Therefore, regularly baste the roast with its cooking juices. If necessary, add to the liquid in the roaster by adding hot water, bouillon, or wine.

3) A roast wrapped in plastic or aluminum foil is almost always a success. The meat browns, but does not dry out. Close the wrapping tightly, then pierce the top several times and set the roast into a cold oven (set oven to 400° at the highest).

| Small Roasts | Very Rare high heat | Rare high heat | Medium medium heat |
|---|---|---|---|
| Entrecote/ London Broil 1 lb. 2 inches thick | 2 to 4 minutes on each side | 3 to 5 minutes on each side | 6 to 8 minutes on each side |
| Entrecote double 1¼ to 2 lb., 3 inches thick | 4 to 6 minutes on each side | 7 to 9 minutes on each side | 10 to 11 minutes on each side |
| Filet Mignon 3 to 4 oz., 1 inch thick | 1½ minutes on each side | 2 to 3 minutes on each side | 3 to 4 minutes on each side |
| Tenderloin Steak ¼ to ⅓ lb. 1 to 1½ inches thick | 1 to 2 minutes on each side | 2 to 3 minutes on each side | 4 to 5 minutes on each side |
| Round Steak ½ lb., 1½ inches thick | 1 to 2 minutes on each side | 2 to 3 minutes on each side | 4 to 5 minutes on each side |
| Porterhouse Steak 2 lb., 2½ to 3 inches thick | 6 to 8 minutes on each side | 8 to 10 minutes on each side | 10 to 12 minutes on each side |
| Beef Medallion ¼ lb., 1½ inches thick | 1 to 2 minutes on each side | 3 to 4 minutes on each side | 4 to 6 minutes on each side |
| Rump Steak ⅓ to ½ lb. 1½ inches thick | 2 to 3 minutes on each side | 4 to 5 minutes on each side | 5 to 7 minutes on each side |
| T-bone Steak 1 to 1¼ lb., 2 inches thick | 3 to 4 minutes on each side | 5 to 6 minutes on each side | 7 to 9 minutes on each side |
| Tournedo under ¼ lb. 1½ to 2 inches thick | 1 to 2 minutes on each side | 3 to 4 minutes on each side | 4 to 6 minutes on each side |
| **Weight** | **2 to 3 oz.** | **4 to 5 oz.** | **6 to 7 oz.** |
| Hamburgers about 1½ inches thick | 4 to 8 minutes depending on type of meat | | 8 to 10 minutes on each side |
| Calf's Liver about 1 inch thick | 1 to 2 minutes on each side | 2 minutes on each side | 3 to 4 minutes on each side |
| Veal Medallion about 1½ inches thick | 2 to 3 minutes on each side | 3 to 4 minutes on each side | 5 to 7 minutes on each side |
| Veal Cutlet about 1½ inches thick | 2 to 3 minutes on each side | 4 to 5 minutes on each side | 6 to 8 minutes on each side |
| Veal Schnitzel about 1 inch thick | 2 to 3 minutes on each side | 4 to 5 minutes on each side | 6 to 8 minutes on each side, breaded |
| Lamb Cutlet about 1½ inches thick | 2 to 3 minutes on each side | 4 to 5 minutes on each side | 6 to 8 minutes on each side |
| Pork Cutlet about 1½ inches thick | 2 to 3 minutes on each side | 4 to 6 minutes on each side | 7 to 8 minutes on each side |
| Pork Schnitzel about 1 inch thick | 2 to 4 minutes on each side | 5 to 6 minutes on each side | 7 to 9 minutes on each side, breaded |

# Sautéed Dishes

# Wiener Schnitzel

**Famous recipe, quick**

Preparation time: 20 minutes

| |
|---|
| 4 veal cutlets (¼ lb. each) |
| ½ tsp. each salt and freshly ground black pepper |
| 1 egg |
| 2 tsp. oil |
| ½ cup bread crumbs |
| 2 tbs. shortening |
| 1 sprig parsley |
| ½ lemon |

**R**inse the cutlets in cold water and dry. Rub the salt and pepper into the meat. • Beat the egg in a large soup bowl, adding the oil and 1 tablespoon water. Pour the bread crumbs onto a flat plate. • Halve the shortening and heat in two pans. • Draw the cutlets through the batter, then dredge in the crumbs; shake off any excess crumbs. • Sauté the cutlets in the heated shortening for 4 minutes on each side, until golden brown. • Garnish with parsley and lemon wedges and serve on warm plates. • Potato salad with cucumber goes well with this.

Tip: If cooking with only 1 frying pan, then be sure to wipe the pan with a paper towel before starting the second pair of schnitzel. Keep the first pair warm in the oven at 350° with the door ajar.

# Cordon Bleu

**Famous recipe**

Preparation time: 30 minutes

| |
|---|
| 4 veal cutlets (⅓ lb. each) |
| ½ tsp. each salt and freshly ground black pepper |
| 4 thin slices cooked ham |
| 4 thin slices Swiss cheese |
| 1 tsp. sweet powdered paprika |
| 4 tbs. flour |
| 2 eggs |
| 6 tbs. bread crumbs |
| 1 tbs. coconut oil |
| 2 tbs. butter |
| ½ lemon |
| 1 sprig parsley |

**R**inse and dry the cutlets, then flatten them a little. Rub the salt and pepper into the cutlets. • Place the ham and cheese on one half of each cutlet and sprinkle the paprika over them. Fold each cutlet over and pin the sides together with toothpicks. • Put the eggs, flour and bread crumbs each into a flat bowl or plate; the eggs should be lightly beaten. • Heat the coconut oil and butter. • Dredge the schnitzel in the flour first, then the egg, and finally in the bread crumbs. • Brown for 6 minutes on each side. • Serve garnished with lemon wedges and the parsley. • Green beans, grilled tomatoes and potato croquettes accompany this dish deliciously.

Tip: The butcher can substitute halved cutlets, that have not been separated on one side, for larger cutlets.

## Schnitzel à la Holstein

**Somewhat more expensive**

Preparation time: 45 minutes

| |
|---|
| 2 tbs. capers |
| 4 thin slices of smoked salmon (about 2 oz.) |
| 1 medium pickle |
| 4 small anchovies |
| ½ lb. sliced red beets (pickled) |
| 4 veal cutlets (¼ lb. each) |
| 4 tbs. butter |
| Salt |
| Freshly ground white pepper |
| 4 eggs |
| 2 tsp. caviar |
| Parsley |
| 4 slices white bread |

Drain the capers. Roll the sliced salmon. Slice the pickle. Pat the anchovies dry. Drain the beets. • Rinse and pat dry the cutlets. • Melt the butter in a skillet. Sauté the cutlets 4 minutes on each side, sprinkling with salt and pepper after turning. Keep warm in a 250° oven. • Fry the eggs sunny side up, then salt. • Arrange the meat and lay one egg on each cutlet. Scatter the capers over the meat and eggs. Arrange the rolled salmon, pickle, anchovies, caviar, and red beets around the meat. Garnish with parsley. Serve with warm toast.

## Veal Cutlet with Tuna Sauce

**Somewhat expensive**

Preparation time: 40 minutes

| |
|---|
| 2 egg yolks |
| 1 lemon |
| 1 tbs. anchovy paste |
| ½ cup olive oil |
| 12 oz. canned tuna (in oil) |
| 2 tbs. small capers |
| 4 tbs. yogurt |
| ½ tsp. each salt and freshly ground white pepper |
| Pinch of sugar |
| 4 veal cutlets (¼ lb. each) |
| 2 tbs. clarified butter |

**B**eat the egg yolks. Rinse and dry the lemon, then halve it, juice one half, combine that with the anchovy paste and the egg yolks. • Whisk the olive oil into the egg mixture, at first drop by drop, then in a thin stream. • Drain the tuna, then puree it with 1 tablespoon capers. • Blend the puree with the yogurt. Add salt, pepper, and sugar to taste. • Rinse and dry the cutlets. Heat the butter in a skillet and sauté the cutlets about 3 minutes on each side. Salt and pepper to taste. • Slice the remaining lemon half. • Arrange the cutlets with the tuna sauce, garnish with a slice of lemon and the remaining capers. • Tomato salad with olives and mozzarella go well with these cutlets.

## Veal Cutlets with Fresh Figs

**Somewhat expensive**

Preparation time: 40 minutes

| 4 veal cutlets (about ⅓ lb. each) |
| ½ tsp. each salt and freshly ground white pepper |
| 4 tbs. port wine |
| ½ cup crème fraîche |
| 2 tbs. lemon juice |
| About 1 tbs. Worcestershire sauce |
| Pinch of cayenne pepper |
| 3 fresh figs |

**R**inse the cutlets and dry. Sauté the cutlets in the butter 4 minutes on each side, salt and pepper, and put aside, covered. • Pour off the fat from the pan and then pour in the port, loosening any scrapings from the bottom of the pan. Add the crème fraîche and simmer gently for 5 minutes. Add the remaining salt, pepper, lemon juice, Worcestershire sauce and cayenne pepper to taste. • Add the cutlets to the sauce and heat. • Rinse the figs, slice and warm them on the cutlets. • Arrange the cutlets and sauce on plates. • Mashed potatoes accompany this well.

## Veal Cutlets with Lemon

**Somewhat difficult**

Preparation time: 50 minutes

| 4 egg whites |
| 4 tbs. lemon juice |
| 7 tbs. soft butter |
| Pinch of sugar |
| ½ tsp. each salt and freshly ground white pepper |
| 4 veal cutlets (⅓ lb. each) |
| 3 tbs. coconut oil |
| ½ tsp. dried sage |
| A little lemon balm |

**I**n a double boiler, stir the egg whites and lemon juice until they are creamy, add the butter in flakes. Add sugar and 1 pinch each salt and pepper. Keep the sauce warm in the double boiler and stir occasionally. • Rinse and dry the cutlets, then make an incision along the bone and flatten the meat somewhat. • Heat the coconut oil, sauté the cutlets 6 minutes on each side, and spice with salt, pepper, and the sage. • Arrange the cutlets with the lemon sauce and garnish with lemon balm. • Serve with fresh French bread.

## Veal Cutlets with Pumpkin

**Easy to prepare**

Preparation time: 50 minutes

2 lb. pumpkin

½ lb. onions

2 tbs. butter

1 tsp. salt

½ tsp. freshly ground white pepper

Pinch of ground anise

3 tbs. lemon juice

½ cup each buttermilk and cream

4 veal cutlets (⅓ lb. each)

½ tsp. freshly ground black pepper

2 egg yolks

2 tbs. milk

2 tbs. freshly grated Parmesan cheese

4 tbs. bread crumbs

3 tbs. clarified butter

4 tbs. flour

½ handful dill

Peel the pumpkin and remove the seeds. Dice the flesh. • Slice the onions into thin rings and sauté these until translucent in the butter. Briefly sauté the diced pumpkin with the onions. Season with ½ teaspoon salt, the white pepper, the anise, and lemon juice, then pour in the buttermilk. Simmer for 15 minutes and add the cream. • Rinse, dry and flatten the cutlets, then make an incision along the bone and salt and pepper the meat. • Beat the yolks and the milk; combine the Parmesan with the bread crumbs. • Heat the clarified butter. • Dredge the cutlets in the flour, eggs and bread crumbs, then sauté 6 minutes on each side in the clarified butter. • Rinse and chop the dill. • Add spices to the pumpkin to taste, arrange it on plates with the cutlets, and sprinkle the dill over both. • New potatoes make the ensemble complete.

## Veal Cutlets with Tomatoes and Olives

**Easy to prepare**

Preparation time: 50 minutes

1 onion

2 tomatoes

½ bunch parsley

3 tbs. olive oil

4 veal cutlets (⅓ to ½ lb. each)

½ tsp. each salt and freshly ground black pepper

4 tbs. stuffed olives

2 cloves of garlic

Chop the onion. Peel, seed and coarsely chop the tomatoes. Rinse the parsley, pick the leaves from the sprigs and chop them. • Heat the oil. Rinse and dry the cutlets, then make an incision along the bone and sauté the veal for 6 minutes on each side. Salt and pepper the cutlets and set them aside. • Sauté the onion in the remaining oil until it is translucent. Add the tomato and olives. Crush the garlic into this mixture, salt and pepper, and cook, covered, for another 10 minutes. • Heat the cutlets in the vegetables, then arrange the meat and vegetables on plates. Sprinkle the parsley over the dish. • Great with home fries.

## Stuffed Veal Cutlets

### Requires some time

Marinating time: 3 hours
Preparation time: 40 minutes

| |
|---|
| 4 veal cutlets (⅓ lb. each) |
| 1 sprig fresh sage |
| Juice of ½ lemon |
| 2 pinches freshly ground black pepper |
| 1 onion |
| ½ lb. mushrooms |
| 1 handful parsley |
| ⅓ cup cream |
| ½ tsp. salt |
| 2 pinches freshly ground white pepper |
| ¼ cup sausage drippings |
| 4 tbs. butter |

**C**ut a pocket into the cutlets on the round side. • Chop the sage and make a marinade with the lemon juice and the black pepper. Marinate the cutlets for 3 hours. • Chop the onion. Slice half of the mushrooms, chop the other half. Chop the parsley. • Simmer the onions and chopped mushrooms in 3 tablespoons cream to form a thick sauce; salt and pepper to taste. Add the parsley and drippings. • Stuff the cutlets with this mixture and close the pockets. • Melt the butter in a frying pan, then sauté the cutlets for 5 minutes on each side (first at high heat, to seal the pores, then at lower heat). Remove from the pan and keep warm. • Cook the mushroom slices and cream for 2 minutes.  Salt and pepper to taste, then pour the sauce over the cutlets and serve. • Cauliflower and mashed potatoes are suggested as side dishes.

## Calf's Liver in White Wine Butter Sauce

**Somewhat difficult, a little expensive**

Preparation time: 50 minutes

| |
|---|
| 2 sprigs fresh tarragon |
| 4 shallots |
| ¼ cup small mushrooms |
| ⅔ cup butter |
| 1½ cups dry white wine |
| ½ tsp. each salt and freshly ground white pepper |
| 1¼ lb. calf's liver |
| 2 tbs. clarified butter |

**R**inse and chop the tarragon. • Chop the shallots. Clean and thinly slice the mushrooms. Cut the butter into small flakes. • Sauté the shallots in 1 tablespoon butter until translucent; pour in the white wine and reduce one third of the liquid. • Whisk in the remaining butter until a creamy sauce is formed. Add salt and pepper. • Add the mushrooms to the sauce. Stew for 5 minutes over low heat and sprinkle in the tarragon. Keep the sauce warm. • Rinse and dry the liver. Sauté in the clarified butter 1 minute on each side, salt and pepper, then arrange on plates. Pour the white wine sauce over the liver. • Savory potato pancakes complement this excellently.

## Calf's Liver with Wheat Sprouts

**Requires some time**

Sprouting time: 2 days
Preparation time: 25 minutes

| |
|---|
| 2 oz. fertile wheat seeds |
| 6 shallots |
| 2 tart apples |
| 4 slices calf's liver (¼ lb. each) |
| Pinch of freshly ground black pepper |
| 3 tbs. butter |
| 2 pinches sea salt |
| ⅓ cup crème fraîche |
| 1 tsp. mustard |
| 1 tbs. each freshly chopped parsley and chives |

**T**wo days before serving this meal, soak the wheat seeds in a little lukewarm water for 2 hours, drain, and allow to sprout in a warm place. • Toss the sprouts every once in a while, cover in a little water mornings and evenings and drain each time. After 2 days, sprouts will have formed. • Slice the shallots into thin rings. Dice the apples. • Rinse and dry the liver, then rub the pepper into it. • Sauté the shallot rings in the butter until translucent. Add the liver and sauté for 2 minutes on each side, along with the diced apple and the sprouts. • Lightly salt the liver. • Pour the crème fraîche into the pan, add salt and mustard to taste, add the herbs, and arrange on plates.

## Veal Roulades with Raisins

**Requires some time**

Soaking time: 30 minutes
Preparation time: 50 minutes

½ cup raisins

1 cup dry white wine

2 thin stalks leek

2 tbs. butter

½ tsp. each salt and freshly ground black pepper

2 tsp. tomato paste

1 tsp. curry powder

8 veal cutlets (3 oz. each)

1 tbs. oil

½ cup cream

Rinse the raisins in warm water and soak them for 30 minutes in the wine. • Trim, rinse, and slice the leek, then sauté briefly in 1 tablespoon butter. Add the drained raisins, salt and pepper, the tomato paste and the curry. Simmer briefly. • Preheat the oven to 250°. • Salt and pepper the cutlets, spread the raisin-leek mixture onto the meat, roll the meat and tie up with kitchen string. • Heat the remaining butter and the oil. Sear the roulades in the fat, then douse them with the soaking wine. Add the cream and simmer over low heat for 10 minutes. • Keep the roulades warm in the oven. • Reduce the sauce by a third, salt and pepper to taste, and serve with the roulades.

## Veal Steaks in Chervil Sauce

**Easy to prepare**

Preparation time: 40 minutes

⅓ cup chervil

4 boned veal cutlets (⅓ lb. each)

2 tbs. butter

1 tbs. oil

½ tsp. each salt and freshly ground white pepper

2 tsp. Dijon mustard

1 cup cream

1 tsp. each lemon juice and soy sauce

Preheat the oven to 250°. • Rinse the chervil and set aside a few leaves. • Rinse the veal, dry, and sauté in the oil and butter for 5 minutes, total. Salt and pepper the veal, spread on the mustard, cover and keep warm. • Heat the chervil in the remaining fat for 1 minute. Bring to a boil with half of the cream, then puree it in a blender. • Pour the sauce into the pan and add lemon juice, soy sauce, salt and pepper to taste. • Whip the remaining cream and fold into the sauce. Pour the chervil sauce over the steaks and garnish with the reserved chervil leaves.

## Peppersteaks Flambé

### Famous recipe

Preparation time: 20 minutes
Serves: 2 people

| |
|---|
| 2 beef fillet steaks (⅓ lb. each) |
| 1 small onion |
| 1 tbs. black peppercorns |
| 2 tbs. oil |
| Pinch of salt for each steak |
| 2 tbs. cognac per steak |
| 1 tbs. butter |

**R**inse and dry the steaks. Cut off any membranes or fat. Bind the steaks with kitchen string to keep the outer edges as thick as the center; this will allow the meat to cook evenly. • Peel and chop the onion. Coarsely grind the peppercorns. • Brush oil on both sides of the steaks and dredge them in the crushed pepper. • Heat the remaining oil and sauté the steaks over high heat for 2 to 3 minutes. Reduce the heat, turn the steaks, add the onion, and sauté until translucent. Sauté the steaks another 2 to 3 minutes, then salt. • Heat the cognac over low heat, pour it over the steaks, light it and let it burn out. • Melt the butter on the steaks. Turn the steaks, then put them on warm plates along with the pan scrapings. Remove the string. • Garlic bread and a green salad complement this wonderfully.

## Tournedos with Herb Butter

### Somewhat expensive

Preparation time: 20 minutes
Cooling time: 1 hour
Cooking time: 12 minutes

| |
|---|
| 5 tbs. butter |
| 2 fresh sprigs each of basil, dill, tarragon, chervil, and parsley |
| 4 fresh sage leaves |
| 1 shallot |
| 1 tsp. salt |
| 4 tournedos (¼ lb. each) |
| 2 tbs. coconut oil |
| ½ tsp. freshly ground white pepper |

**C**ut the butter into small pieces. • Rinse and dry the herbs, pick out any tough stems, and coarsely chop the leaves. • Peel and grate the shallot. • Mix the butter until it is creamy, blend with ½ teaspoon salt, the shallot and the herbs. Make a 1-inch roll and wrap in waxed paper; refrigerate for 1 hour. • Rinse, dry and bind the tournedos with kitchen string, to make the edges as thick as the middle. • Heat the oil and sauté the tournedos for 3 to 4 minutes on each side. Reduce the heat once the steaks are in the pan. • Salt and pepper the steaks after searing. • Cut the herb butter into 8 slices. • Arrange the meat and place the butter on top. • Cooked fennel and French bread go well with these steaks.

# T-Bone Steaks with Sour Cream

**Somewhat expensive, famous recipe**

Preparation time: 50 minutes

| |
|---|
| 4 large potatoes |
| 1½ cups sour cream |
| 1 small onion |
| 1 clove of garlic |
| 1 handful each of dill and chives |
| Salt |
| Pinch of freshly ground white pepper |
| 1-2 tbs. herb vinegar |
| 2 T-bone steaks (a little under 1 lb. each) |
| 2 tbs. clarified butter |
| 2 pinches freshly ground black pepper |
| 2 tomatoes |
| Parsley |

**P**reheat the oven to 425°. • Brush the potatoes under running water, wrap each in a piece of strong aluminum foil, and bake in the oven for 45 minutes. • Blend the chopped onion and crushed garlic into the sour cream. • Rinse and drain the herbs, chop them, and combine with the sour cream. Add salt, pepper, and vinegar to taste. • Rinse and dry the meat. Heat the clarified butter in two skillets, sauté the steaks for 7 to 9 minutes on each side, then salt and pepper them. • Open the foil on the potatoes. Use a kitchen towel to hold the hot potatoes, press each one in order to open its skin, then put two tablespoons sour cream on each. • Carve the steaks, arrange on plates with the potatoes, and garnish with tomato wedges and parsley. • Serve any remaining sour cream separately.

## Rump Steak with Mushrooms

**Somewhat expensive**

Preparation time: 1 hour

1 handful mixed herbs, chervil, tarragon, parsley, chives

1 clove of garlic

¼ lb. soft butter

½ tsp. each salt and freshly ground white pepper

½ lb. mushrooms

1 large white onion

4 rump steaks (½ lb. each)

4 tbs. oil

½ tsp. paprika

1 handful parsley

5 tbs. dry red wine

**R**inse the herbs, chop them together with the garlic, blend with a pinch of salt and pepper, and 6 tablespoons of the butter. Roll the herb butter in waxed paper and refrigerate. • Preheat the oven to 250°. • Clean and halve the mushrooms. Finely chop the onion. • Rinse and dry the steaks, then make several cuts in the fatty edge. • Heat the oil, then sear each side of the steaks for 1 minute and continue sautéing at a lower heat for 3 minutes on each side. Sprinkle salt, pepper, and paprika over the steaks and keep them warm in the oven. • Sauté the chopped onion in the oil until translucent; add the mushrooms and continue until the liquid has evaporated. • Chop the parsley and add it with the red wine and the remaining butter to the mushrooms. • Put pats of the herb butter on the steaks and serve with the mushrooms.

## Rump Steak with Garlic Sauce

**Somewhat expensive**

Preparation time: 50 minutes

2 cloves of garlic

3 egg yolks

½ cup herb oil or olive oil

½ tsp. each of salt and freshly ground white pepper

Pinch of sugar

1 tbs. lemon juice

2 tbs. chopped chives

4 rump steaks (½ lb. each)

4 tbs. oil

½ tsp. dried rosemary

**C**rush the garlic cloves. • Beat the egg yolks, adding the oil drop by drop at first, then in a thin stream. Blend in 1 pinch of salt and pepper, the sugar, lemon juice, garlic and chives. • Rinse and dry the steaks, then make several incisions along the fatty side. • Heat the oil and sauté the steaks 4 minutes on each side over high heat. Sprinkle the rosemary, salt and pepper over the steaks. • Arrange the steaks and pour the drippings and garlic sauce over them. • Potato croquettes and grilled tomatoes taste great with these steaks.

## Tournedos with Sherry Sabayon

**Somewhat difficult, quick**

Preparation time: 30 minutes

| 4 tournedos from beef fillet (¼ lb. each) |
| 2 tbs. clarified butter |
| ½ tsp. each salt and freshly ground black pepper |
| Pinch of hot paprika powder |
| 3 egg yolks |
| 1 cup beef broth |
| ½ cup dry sherry |
| 1 tbs. lemon juice |

**P**reheat the oven to 250°. • Sauté the tournedos 4 minutes on each side in the clarified butter, turning them frequently, then lightly season with salt and pepper, and place, covered, in the oven for 15 minutes. • Blend the paprika powder with the egg yolks and a little salt and pepper, then whip in a double boiler. • Blend the beef broth and sherry, stir into the egg yolks until a creamy sauce forms. Add lemon juice to taste. • Arrange the tournedos on plates and pour the sherry sabayon around them. • Potatoes and a chicory salad with kiwis accompany this deliciously.

## Tenderloin with Herbed-Marrow Crust

**Somewhat expensive, requires some time**

Preparation time: 50 minutes

| 2 large marrow bones |
| 1½ lb. well aged tenderloin |
| 3 tbs. clarified butter |
| 1 tsp. each salt and freshly ground black pepper |
| Pinch of freshly grated nutmeg |
| 2 handfuls parsley |
| 1 handful basil |
| 3 cloves of garlic |
| 7 tbs. bread crumbs |

**R**emove the marrow from the bones. • Rinse and dry the loin, then sear all sides in the clarified butter, at first over high heat, then at a medium heat. Sprinkle with salt, pepper, and nutmeg, remove from heat and set aside, covered, for 15 minutes. • Preheat the oven to 475°. • Rinse, dry, and chop the herbs. Crush the garlic into the herbs. Add the bread crumbs. • Dice the marrow, combine with the herbs, salt and pepper, then spread it onto the meat. • Lay the loin onto aluminum foil, place it on the middle rack of the oven and bake until golden brown. • Carve the loin. • Serve with new potatoes and peas.

## Round Steaks with Soybean Sprouts

**Nutritious, quick**

Preparation time: 30 minutes

¼ lb. soybean sprouts

1 bunch green onions

4 round steaks (a little over ¼ lb. each)

½ tsp. freshly ground black pepper

1 tbs. oil

Sea salt

2 tbs. butter

1 tbs. soy sauce

1 tbs. crème fraîche

1 tbs. cognac

**B**lanch the sprouts in a sieve for 3 minutes, then drain. • Rinse, halve and cut the onions into 1 inch pieces. • Rinse the steaks, dry, and rub the pepper into them. • Brush a broiling pan with oil. Lay the steaks on the broiling pan and broil them under high heat for 3 minutes on each side, then salt, cover and keep warm. • Melt the butter and sauté the sprouts and onions for about 5 minutes, remove from heat and add the soy sauce, crème fraîche and cognac. Salt to taste and arrange the vegetables with the steaks. • Baked potatoes go well with this.

## Sirloin Steaks with Mustard Sprouts

**Nutritious, takes some time**

Sprouting time: 5 days
Preparation time: 20 minutes

1 tbs. fertile mustard seeds

4 large onions

4 tbs. oil

4 sirloin steaks (a little over ¼ lb. each)

2 pinches each sea salt and freshly ground black pepper

⅓-½ cup cream

1 tbs. mustard

**A**t least 5 days before making this dish, start the sprouts. • After 5 days, cut the sprouts from the seeds with a pair of scissors, rinse, and drain. • Peel and thinly slice the onions. Sauté them in the oil until they are golden brown, remove from the pan with a slotted spoon, and put aside on a warm plate. • Rinse and dry the steaks, then rub the pepper into them. • Reheat the oil and sauté the steaks for 4 minutes on each side, arrange with the onions, and salt. • Use the cream to help loosen the scrapings, blend with the mustard, salt to taste, and pour over the steaks. Sprinkle the sprouts over the steaks.

## Fillet Steaks with Gorgonzola Cheese

**Somewhat expensive, quick**

Preparation time: 30 minutes

| |
|---|
| 1¼ lb. beef fillet |
| 2 tbs. clarified butter |
| 2 pinches freshly ground black pepper |
| 4 oz. Gorgonzola or other mild blue cheese |
| 2 tbs. cream cheese |

**P**reheat the oven to 475°. • Slice the fillet into 4 equal pieces. Rinse and dry the slices. • Heat the clarified butter in a large skillet. Lay the fillet slices into the fat and reduce the heat to medium. Sauté the meat 2 to 3 minutes on each side. Remove the steaks from the skillet, pepper, and set aside, covered. • Mash the cheese with a fork and blend with the cream cheese to a smooth creamy consistency. • Lay the steaks next to one another on a cookie pan and spread the cheese evenly over all pieces. • Bake the steaks on the top rack of the oven until the cheese is melted and just brown. • French bread and a tossed salad accompany these steaks very nicely.

## Fillet Steaks with Pureed Mushrooms

**Somewhat expensive**

Preparation time: 50 minutes

| |
|---|
| ½ lb. mushrooms |
| 3 tbs. oil |
| 2 shallots |
| 1 tbs. butter |
| 4 tenderloin steaks (about ¼ lb. each) |
| 1 tsp. each salt and freshly ground white pepper |
| 3 tbs. crème fraîche |
| 1 tbs. Worcestershire sauce |
| 1 tsp. grated lemon rind |
| 1 tsp. lemon juice |
| 3 green onions |

**C**lean and rinse the mushrooms, cut into strips, sauté in 1 tablespoon oil, and stew in their liquid for 15 minutes. • Peel, finely chop, and add the shallots to the mushrooms, then puree the mixture. • Heat the remaining oil and butter, sauté the steaks for 2 to 3 minutes on each side, then remove the steaks. Salt and pepper them, then wrap them in aluminum foil and set aside for 15 minutes. • Return the mushroom puree to the pan, blend in the crème fraîche and simmer gently for 5 minutes. Add salt, pepper, Worcestershire sauce, lemon rind and juice to taste. • Clean and rinse the green onions, slice them into thin rings, then add them to the puree. • Add the steaks and their juices to the puree. • Dumplings are great with this dish.

## Chateaubriand with Grapefruit Sauce

**Somewhat expensive**

Preparation time: 45 minutes
Cooking time: 30 minutes

| |
|---|
| 2 pink grapefruits |
| ½ cup soft butter |
| ½ tsp. each salt and freshly ground white pepper |
| 1 tbs. soy sauce |
| Pinch of cayenne pepper |
| 2 tbs. oil |
| 1½ lb. well aged tenderloin |
| 1 bunch garden cress |

Juice one of the grapefruits, peel, fillet, and refrigerate the other. • Blend the grapefruit juice with the butter and with half the salt, half the pepper, the soy sauce and the cayenne pepper. Refrigerate for at least 30 minutes. • Preheat the oven to 350°. • Heat the oil in a roaster, sear the meat on all sides, cover the roaster, and put it in the oven to roast for 25 minutes. • Salt and pepper the meat, wrap it in aluminum foil, and keep warm in the oven. • Discard the roasting fat. Melt the butter and juice mixture in a pan, reduce by a third over low heat, and add spices to taste. • Heat the grapefruit segments in the sauce. Cut off the cress leaves, rinse, drain, and scatter over the sauce. • Carve the meat and pour the sauce over it. • Egg noodles soak up the sauce well.

## Entrecote with Avocado Sauce

**Somewhat expensive, easy to prepare**

Preparation time: 45 minutes

| |
|---|
| 4 thin entrecotes (tenderloin steaks of ⅓ lb. each) |
| 3 tbs. clarified butter |
| 1 tsp. each salt and freshly ground white pepper |
| 2 ripe avocados |
| Juice of 1 lemon |
| 3 tbs. heavy cream |
| Pinch of cayenne pepper |
| 2 tbs. chopped chives |

**R**inse and dry the steaks, then sear in the clarified butter for 3 minutes on each side. Sprinkle salt and pepper on the steaks, then set aside on a warm, covered plate. • Peel, halve, and pit the avocados. Sprinkle lemon juice over the fruit to avoid discoloration. • Set aside ½ of an avocado; in a blender, puree the other 3 halves with the heavy cream. • Clean out the skillet and pour the avocado sauce into it. Heat the sauce, but do not let it come to a boil. Add salt, pepper, and cayenne pepper to taste. • Warm the meat and its juices in the sauce. Sprinkle the chives into the sauce. • Slice the remaining avocado half into wedges and sprinkle lemon juice over them. • Arrange the meat and sauce on warm plates and garnish with avocado wedges. • Buttered rice goes well with these steaks.

## Porterhouse Steak in Mustard Sauce

**Somewhat expensive, famous recipe**

Preparation time: 50 minutes

| |
|---|
| 1 porterhouse steak (1½ lb.) |
| 3 tbs. oil |
| 1 tsp. each salt and freshly ground black pepper |
| ½ tsp. dried thyme |
| 2 shallots |
| 1 cup dry white wine |
| 5 tbs. Dijon mustard |
| 3 tbs. crème fraîche |
| Pinch of cayenne pepper |

**P**reheat the oven to 250°. • Rinse and dry the steak. Sear in the oil for 3 minutes on each side, then sauté for another 10 minutes over medium heat. Salt, pepper, and sprinkle the thyme over the steak. • Wrap the steak in aluminum foil and keep warm in the oven for 15 minutes. • Peel and chop the shallots, sauté in the drippings until translucent. Douse the shallots with the white wine and simmer until reduced by half. • Whisk the mustard and crème fraîche into this sauce. Simmer gently for 5 minutes and add salt, pepper, and cayenne to taste. • Cut the meat into strips, cutting across the grain. Add any juices to the sauce. • Arrange the meat on a preheated platter and pour the sauce over it. • Glazed carrots and fresh potatoes go well with this dish.

## Venison Medallions with Fruit

**Somewhat expensive**

Preparation time: 45 minutes

| |
| --- |
| ⅔ lb. fresh pineapple |
| 1 large orange |
| 1 banana |
| 1 large tart apple |
| 2 tbs. lemon juice |
| 2 tbs. Cointreau |
| 1¼ lb. venison fillet |
| 4 slices white bread |
| 4 tbs. butter |
| ½ tsp. salt |
| ½ tsp. freshly ground white pepper |

**P**eel, core and dice the pineapple. Peel the orange and cut into pieces. Peel and slice the banana and apple. • Sprinkle the lemon juice and Cointreau over the fruits and set aside, covered. • Rinse, dry and trim the membranes from the venison. Slice the meat into 4 equal pieces and flatten the pieces with the palm of the hand. • Trim the bread to fit the fillets. • Melt two tablespoons butter and brown both sides of the bread in it. • Preheat the oven to 425°. Warm the plates and keep the bread warm on them. • Melt the remaining butter, sauté the venison for 3 minutes on each side and sprinkle with salt and pepper after turning the meat. The meat should still be pink inside. • Arrange the venison on the bread, pour the drippings over the meat and arrange the fruit next to it.

## Venison Cutlet Flambé

**Somewhat expensive, famous recipe**

Marinating time: 2 hours
Preparation time: 30 minutes

| |
| --- |
| 4 venison cutlets (¼ lb. each) |
| 2 tbs. walnut oil |
| 1 tsp. dried rosemary |
| 2 kiwis |
| 1 tbs. butter |
| 4 walnuts |
| ½ tsp. salt |
| ½ tsp. freshly ground white pepper |
| 2 tbs. cognac |

**R**inse and dry the venison, remove all membranes, then rub the oil into the meat. • Crush the rosemary, sprinkle it over the venison, stack the cutlets, wrap them in aluminum foil, and marinate in the refrigerator for 2 hours. • Peel and slice the kiwis, warm them in the melted butter, but do not brown. • Coarsely chop the walnuts. • Heat a heavy skillet, sauté the venison for 2 to 3 minutes on each side, then salt, pepper, and arrange on plates. • Warm the cognac and pour it over the cutlets. Flambé the venison. • Croquettes go well with this.

## Venison Steaks with Mushrooms

### Somewhat expensive

Marinating time: 4 hours
Preparation time: 35 minutes

| |
|---|
| 1½ lb. fillet of venison |
| 6 juniper berries |
| 6 white peppercorns |
| 1 tsp. dried thyme |
| ½ tsp. black peppercorns |
| ½ cup sherry or port wine |
| 4 shallots |
| 1 handful chervil |
| 1 lb. mushrooms |
| 4 slices bacon |
| Salt and freshly ground white pepper |
| 3 tbs. butter |
| 2 tbs. oil |
| ⅔ cup cream |

Rinse and dry the fillet, cut it into 8 slices and flatten. • Crush the juniper berries and white peppercorns and combine with the thyme and black peppercorns. • Dredge the steaks in this mixture, pour 3 tablespoons port wine over them and marinate, covered, for 4 hours; turn them often. • Chop the shallots and chervil. Dice the bacon. Clean and slice the mushrooms. • Fry the bacon, sauté ½ of the shallots and all of the mushrooms with the bacon for 1 minute, then sprinkle salt and pepper over them. Braise for 5 minutes and keep warm. • Sear the steaks in the butter and oil for 3 minutes on each side, salt and keep warm. • Put the remaining shallots, port, and the cream into the pan with the meat drippings, reduce a bit, and salt and pepper to taste. • Arrange the steaks, cover them with the mushrooms and pour the sauce around them. • Noodles and cranberry sauce make this meal complete.

## Lamb Cutlets with Green Rye

**Nutritious, quick**

Preparation time: 15 minutes
Cooking time: 30 minutes

| |
|---|
| 1 onion |
| 1 lb. young green beans |
| 2 tbs. olive oil |
| 1 cup coarsely ground green rye |
| 1 tsp. vegetable broth |
| 1 tsp. summer savory |
| ½ tsp. basil |
| 3 pinches freshly ground black pepper |
| 4 butterfly lamb cutlets (⅓ lb. each) |
| 2 tbs. oil |
| ½ tsp. salt |
| 4 tbs. dry red wine |
| 1 tomato |

**D**ice the onion. • Trim, rinse and halve the beans. • Heat the oil, sauté the onion and green rye until the onion is translucent and the rye is mottled. • Add the beans, 1½ cups water, the vegetable broth, the herbs and a pinch of pepper. Stew for 25 minutes over low heat. • Rinse the cutlets, dry, and make incisions in the fatty edge about every 2 inches. Rub pepper into the meat. • Heat the oil, sauté the meat for 3 to 4 minutes on each side. • Drain the beans, combine with the rye and arrange the vegetables on a warmed platter. Arrange the cutlets next to the vegetables and salt lightly. • Loosen the pan scrapings by pouring the red wine over them, then pour this over the meat and garnish the platter with tomato slices.

## Lamb Cutlets with Sage

**Quick, easy to prepare**

Preparation time: 30 minutes

| 4 butterfly lamb cutlets (⅓ lb. each) |
| ½ tsp. freshly ground black pepper |
| 1 clove of garlic |
| 4 tbs. oil |
| ½ tsp. salt |
| ½ cup dry red wine |
| 2 sprigs fresh sage |

**R**inse and dry the cutlets, then make several incisions in the fatty edge of the meat.

Rub pepper into the meat. • Peel and crush the garlic, then spread over the cutlets. • Preheat the oven to 250°. • Heat the oil in a large skillet. Sauté 2 cutlets at a time over high heat for 3 minutes on each side, salt and keep warm in the oven. • Loosen the scrapings with the red wine and reduce somewhat. • Pick the sage leaves from the sprigs, rinse, dry, cut into thin strips and add to the sauce. Pour the sauce over the cutlets. • Serve with green beans and croquettes.

## Lamb Cutlets with Feta Cheese

**Easy to prepare, quick**

Preparation time: 30 minutes

| 4 butterfly lamb cutlets (⅓ lb. each) |
| 2 cloves of garlic |
| ½ tsp. freshly ground black pepper |
| 4 tbs. olive oil |
| ½ tsp. salt |
| ¼ lb. feta cheese |
| 1 tbs. each freshly chopped thyme and oregano or ½ tsp. each dried herbs |

**P**reheat the oven to 425°. • Rinse and dry the cutlets, then make several incisions in

the fatty edge. • Peel the cloves of garlic, crush, combine with the pepper, and rub the mixture into the meat. • Heat the olive oil in a large skillet and sauté the cutlets in it over high heat for 3 minutes on each side, then salt. • Crumble the cheese and combine with the herbs. • Lay the meat on a broiling pan, scatter the cheese over the meat, then slide the pan onto the top rack of the oven and bake until the cheese is golden brown, about 7 minutes. • Grilled tomatoes spiced with oregano and French bread are served with this dish.

## Lamb Cutlets with Garlic-Cream Sauce

**Famous recipe, quick**

Preparation time: 30 minutes

| |
|---|
| 1 ripe avocado |
| 1 tsp. salt |
| 4 cloves of garlic |
| ½ cup cream |
| 2 tbs. finely chopped basil |
| 4 butterfly lamb cutlets (¼ lb. each) |
| 1 tbs. butter |
| ½ tsp. freshly ground white pepper |
| 1 tbs. flour |
| 2 tbs. clarified butter |

**H**alve the avocado lengthwise, pit, spoon the flesh out of the halves, strain it through a sieve and combine ½ teaspoon salt and the crushed garlic with the mass. • Whip the cream and add with the basil to the avocado, then place the mixture in the refrigerator. • Rinse and dry the cutlets, then remove any large portions of fat. Cut 2½ inches of meat away from the bone. • Melt the butter. Rub the remaining salt and the pepper into the meat, then draw the meat through the butter and the flour. • Heat the clarified butter and sauté the cutlets over high heat for 3 minutes on each side. • Arrange the cutlets for serving and pour the garlic-cream sauce over them. • Broccoli is suggested as an accompanying dish.

## Lamb Medallions with Stuffed Tomatoes

**Somewhat more expensive**

Preparation time: 40 minutes

| |
|---|
| ½ cup beef broth |
| 8 small ripe tomatoes |
| 1 tsp. salt |
| 4 lamb medallions (¼ lb. each) |
| 5 tbs. butter |
| ½ tsp. sweet powdered paprika |
| 4 tbs. freshly grated Swiss cheese |
| 4 tbs. wheat germ oil |
| 4 tbs. finely crumbled zwieback |

**P**reheat the oven to 440°. • Heat the broth. • Rinse the tomatoes and make a cut on the round end about half way into the flesh. Squeeze apart the opening and sprinkle salt into each pocket. • Place the tomatoes in a small casserole and pour in the broth; bake them for 10 minutes. • Rinse, dry and trim the meat, then flatten it slightly with the palm of the hand and bind it into shape with kitchen string. • Melt 2 tablespoons butter. Rub the remaining salt and the paprika into the meat, then draw it through the butter. • Sprinkle 1 teaspoon grated cheese over each tomato, lay a flake of butter on each and brown in the oven for another 10 minutes. • Heat the oil. Dredge the meat in the zwieback crumbs, then sauté over medium heat for 3 minutes on each side. • Arrange the medallions and tomatoes for serving. • Garlic bread goes well with this.

## Ground Lamb with Anchovy Sauce

**Requires some time**

Preparation time: 1 hour

| |
|---|
| 1 day-old roll |
| 1¼ lb. ground lamb |
| 1 large onion |
| 4 tbs. butter |
| 3 cloves garlic |
| 2 bundles parsley |
| 1 egg |
| 1 egg yolk |
| 1 tsp. each salt and freshly ground black pepper |
| 1 tsp. grated lemon rind |
| 1 tsp. dried oregano |
| 1 pinch cayenne pepper |
| 3 tbs. oil |
| 3 tbs. capers |
| ½ cup dry white wine |
| 2 anchovy fillets |
| 4 tbs. crème fraîche |
| Juice of ½ lemon |

Soak the roll in cold water, squeeze out the water and add the bread to the ground meat. • Preheat the oven to 250°. • Finely chop the onion and sauté it in 2 tablespoons butter until translucent. Crush the garlic into the onion. • Chop the parsley and add it to the onion. • Combine this mixture with the egg, egg yolk, spices and ground meat and knead well. • Make small meatballs out of the ground meat, flatten them somewhat, and sauté in the heated oil until golden brown. • Place the cooked patties into the oven to keep warm. • Melt the remaining butter and pour 2 tablespoons capers, the white wine, the anchovy and the crème fraîche into the pan to make a sauce. Simmer gently for 10 minutes, then puree the sauce in a blender. • Stir the remaining capers and the lemon juice into the sauce and serve with the lamb patties. • It is suggested that pita bread with sesame be served with this.

## Pork Cutlets on Potatoes au Gratin

### Requires some time

Preparation time: 30 minutes
Cooking time: 1 hour

| |
|---|
| 1 lb. cooking potatoes |
| 2 onions |
| 2 tbs. shortening |
| 1 tsp. each salt and freshly ground black pepper |
| 1 tsp. dried thyme |
| 1 cup beef broth |
| 4 pork cutlets (⅓ lb. each) |
| 1 handful parsley |
| 2 cloves of garlic |
| 7 tbs. crème fraîche |

Preheat the oven to 400°. •
Peel, rinse and thinly slice
the potatoes. • Peel and slice the
onions into thin rings. • Melt half
of the shortening in a gratin dish.
Layer the potato slices and onion
rings in the dish. Sprinkle salt,
pepper, and thyme on each
layer. • Pour the broth over the
potatoes, wrap aluminum foil
over the dish and bake for 40
minutes. • Rinse and dry the cutlets, make several incisions in the
edges, sauté in the remaining
shortening for 2 minutes on each
side over high heat, and salt and
pepper. • Rinse and chop the
parsley. Peel and crush the garlic,
and combine with the parsley
and crème fraîche. Salt and pepper to taste. • Arrange the cutlets
on the gratin, pour the herb-
cream sauce over them and
brown in the oven 20 minutes. •
Serve with a green salad.

## Provençal Cutlets

**Inexpensive, easy to prepare**

Preparation time: 30 minutes

| |
| --- |
| 4 pork cutlets (⅓ lb. each) |
| 8 tbs. olive oil |
| 1 handful parsley |
| 2 cloves of garlic |
| ½ tsp. each dried rosemary and thyme |
| 2 tbs. bread crumbs |
| ½ tsp. each salt and freshly ground black pepper |

**R**inse and dry the cutlets, then make a 2½-inch incision along the bone and make several cuts into the fatty edge. • Heat 3 tablespoons oil and sauté the cutlets over high heat for 4 minutes on each side. • Preheat the oven to 425°. • Rinse, dry and chop the parsley. • Peel and crush the garlic, then combine it with the parsley, rosemary, thyme, bread crumbs and the remaining olive oil. • Salt and pepper the meat, spread the herbal mixture on it and brown in the oven. • Corn and stewed tomatoes are suggested as side dishes.

## Cutlets with Apples and Calvados

**Easy to prepare**

Preparation time: 40 minutes

| |
| --- |
| 2 onions |
| 2 small apples |
| 4 pork cutlets (⅓ lb. each) |
| 3 tbs. shortening |
| ½ tsp. each salt and freshly ground black pepper |
| 1 tsp. dried marjoram |
| 3 tbs. apple brandy |
| ½ handful parsley |

**P**reheat the oven to 250°. • Peel the onions and slice with a grater. • Peel, quarter, core and slice the apples. • Rinse and dry the cutlets; cut the meat away from the bone and make several incisions along the fatty edges. • Heat the shortening, sauté the cutlets in it for 4 minutes on each side over high heat, salt, pepper, and sprinkle marjoram over the meat. Keep the cutlets warm in the oven. • Sauté the onion rings in the remaining grease for 5 minutes. Douse the rings with the brandy and spice with the remaining salt, pepper, and marjoram. • Rinse and chop the parsley, sprinkle it over the apples, then cover the cutlets with the apples. • Mashed potatoes go nicely with this dish.

## Pork Schnitzel with Cheese Breading

**Inexpensive, quick**

Preparation time: 20 minutes

¼ cup Swiss cheese

½ tsp. dried oregano

½ tsp. freshly ground white pepper

¼ cup bread crumbs

2 eggs

4 tbs. flour

4 thin pork cutlets (¼ to ⅓ lb. each)

½ tsp. salt

3 tbs. butter

5 tbs. oil

1 lemon

**F**inely grate the cheese. Grind the oregano, then combine with the cheese and add the bread crumbs and pepper. • Beat the eggs and pour the flour onto a plate. • Rinse and dry the cutlets, then sprinkle the salt on them. • Heat the butter and oil. • Dredge the cutlets in the flour, then draw them through the egg batter (allowing excess egg to drip off), and finally dredge in the bread crumbs. Shake off any loose crumbs. • Sauté the cutlets in hot oil and butter over medium heat for 4 to 5 minutes on each side. • Rinse the lemon in warm water and slice 4 thin slices from the middle of the fruit. • Serve the cutlets garnished with the lemon slices.

## Pork Schnitzel in Paprika Cream

**Inexpensive, easy to prepàre**

Preparation time: 50 minutes

3 small red bell peppers

1 onion

2 cloves of garlic

4 pork cutlets (¼ to ⅓ lb. each)

1 tbs. oil

2 tbs. butter

½ tsp. each salt and freshly ground black pepper

1 tbs. sweet paprika

1 tsp. hot paprika

¾ cup cream

**H**alve the bell peppers, remove all membranes, seeds and stem parts, rinse, dry, and slice into thin strips. • Peel the onion and garlic and finely chop. • Rinse and dry the meat. • Heat the oil and butter. Sauté the pork over high heat for 4 minutes on each side, salt and pepper, set aside and cover with aluminum foil. • Sauté the onion and garlic with ⅔ of the bell peppers in the remaining fat. Salt and pepper the vegetables, add the paprika, bring to a boil with 1 cup water and then puree in the blender. • Pour the puree into the pan and bring to a boil with the cream and remaining bell pepper. • Warm the meat with any juices in the sauce. • Egg noodles will soak up the sauce.

## Pork Medallions with Avocado Sauce

### Somewhat more expensive

Preparation time: 30 minutes

| |
| --- |
| 1¼ lb. pork fillet |
| 1 clove of garlic |
| ½ tsp. freshly ground black pepper |
| ½ tsp. sweet paprika |
| ½ tsp. curry powder |
| 3 tbs. oil |
| 1 tsp. salt |
| 1 leek |
| ½ cup dry white wine |
| 2 ripe avocados |
| 2 tbs. crème fraîche |
| 1 sprig lemon balm |

Preheat the oven to 250°. • Rinse and dry the meat. • Peel and crush the garlic, then combine it with the other spices. • Cut the meat into 1-inch thick slices, flatten slightly and rub the spice mixture into it. • Heat the oil, sauté the medallions over medium heat for 5 minutes on each side, then salt them and place in the oven to keep warm. • Remove the dark leaf tips and the bitter root from the leek, halve, rinse, and chop. • Stir the leek in the hot oil, then douse with the wine and simmer until the liquid has evaporated. • Peel, halve, and pit the avocados. Mash the flesh with a fork and blend with the crème fraîche and the leek. Salt and pepper to taste. • Arrange the puree next to the meat and garnish with lemon balm.

## Pork Medallions with Julienned Carrots

### Easy to prepare

Preparation time: 50 minutes

| |
| --- |
| ½ lb. carrots |
| ¼ lb. celeriac |
| 1 onion |
| 1¼ lb. pork fillet |
| ½ tsp. curry powder |
| ½ tsp. dried thyme |
| 2 tbs. coconut oil |
| 1 tsp. salt |
| 2 tbs. soy sauce |
| ½ cup beef broth |
| 2 tsp. cornstarch |
| 1 tbs. lemon juice |
| Pinch of sugar |
| Pinch of cayenne pepper |
| 2 tbs. chopped parsley |

Peel, rinse and julienne the carrots. Peel, rinse and similarly slice the celeriac. Peel and chop the onion. • Preheat the oven to 250°. • Rinse and dry the meat, then cut into 8 slices, flatten slightly and rub the thyme and curry into it. • Sauté the medallions in the oil over high heat for 4 to 5 minutes on each side, then salt and keep warm in the oven. • Sauté the carrots, celeriac, and onion in the remaining grease, pour the soy sauce and broth into the pan and simmer gently for 5 minutes. • Blend the starch and lemon juice, then stir this into the sauce. Add spices to taste. • Add the parsley to the vegetables. • Arrange the vegetables next to the medallions. • Serve with warm French bread.

## Turkish Kabobs

**Requires some time**

Marinating time: 4 hours
Preparation time: 25 minutes

1¼ lb. lean tender mutton

5 tbs. olive oil

2 pinches freshly ground black pepper

1 tbs. each freshly chopped parsley and peppermint

4 slices bacon

Rinse and dry the meat, remove any fat and membranes and cut into pieces 2 inches wide and ½ inch thick. • Mix the oil with the pepper and herbs. Dredge the meat through this mixture and marinate, covered, in the refrigerator for 4 hours. • Cut the bacon into 2 inch pieces. Stick the meat and bacon onto skewers, alternating the two meats. • Heat a broiling pan large enough to hold the skewers. • Roast the skewers 12 to 15 minutes, turning often and basting with the marinade. • Rice Pilaf and tomato salad go well with this dish.

Tip: Further heighten the flavorful experience of kabobs by adding onions and bell peppers to the skewers.

## Fillet Skewers with Plums

**Requires some time**

Preparation time: 1¼ hours

½ lb. plums (pitted)

½ cup dry white wine

1 tsp. white peppercorns

1 clove

1 tsp. coriander seeds

1 small chili pepper

1 tsp. salt

1 lb. pork fillet

½ tsp. freshly ground black pepper

1 tsp. medium paprika powder

3 tbs. clarified butter

Simmer the plums, wine, peppercorns, clove, coriander, chili pepper, and some salt for 10 minutes, remove from heat and marinate for 30 minutes. • Rinse and dry the meat, then cut it into cubes of about the same size as the plums. Rub salt, pepper, and paprika powder into the meat. • Drain the plums, pat dry and skewer, alternating with the meat. • Heat the clarified butter in a sufficiently large pan and broil the skewers until they are brown. • Serve with curry rice.

## Grilled Spare Ribs

**Takes some time, an American specialty**

Preparation time: 15 minutes
Marinating time: 1 hour
Cooking time: 40 minutes

| |
|---|
| 4 tbs. honey |
| 4 tbs. tomato paste |
| 1 tbs. soy sauce |
| 4 cloves of garlic |
| ½ tsp. each salt and freshly ground black pepper |
| Pinch of paprika |
| 4 lb. spare ribs |
| 2 tbs. oil |

**H**eat the honey in a small pan until it is liquid. • Add the tomato paste and soy sauce to the honey. Peel and crush the garlic into the sauce. Spice with salt, pepper and some paprika powder. • Rinse and dry the spare ribs, then rub the remaining salt and pepper into the meat, spread the sauce onto the meat and wrap it in aluminum foil. Marinate, refrigerated, for 1 hour. • Grill the spare ribs on oiled aluminum foil for 30 to 40 minutes, depending on the size of the pieces of meat; turn frequently. • Fresh bread and cucumber salad are suggested as side dishes.

Tip: Spare ribs are not necessarily available at all meat departments or butchers, so order them a day ahead of time, just to be sure.

## Burgers with Vegetables

**Easy to prepare, inexpensive**

Preparation time: 1 hour

| |
|---|
| 2 large onions |
| 1 egg |
| 2 tsp. sweet paprika powder |
| ½ tsp. each salt and freshly ground black pepper |
| Pinch of dried marjoram |
| 4 tbs. bread crumbs |
| Dash of Worcestershire sauce |
| ⅔ lb. ground meat |
| 4 tbs. shortening |
| 2 slices bacon |
| 2 large potatoes |
| ½ cup hot beef broth |
| 1 red bell pepper |
| 1 zucchini |
| ⅔ lb. hulled peas |
| 2 tbs. chopped chives |

Peel the onions. Slice one into rings, chop the other. • Knead the chopped onion, egg, spices, bread crumbs, and Worcestershire sauce into the meat. • Preheat the oven to 250°. • Make 4 burgers and sauté for 8 minutes on each side in 3 tablespoons of shortening over medium heat; keep warm in the oven. • Dice the bacon and fry in the remaining grease until it is crisp. • Peel, dice and sauté the potatoes with the onion rings in the bacon grease. Add the beef broth and simmer gently for 10 minutes. • Rinse, trim and slice the bell pepper and the zucchini. Add these vegetables and the peas to the potatoes and cook for another 5 minutes. Sprinkle the chives over the vegetables when done.

## Chinese Burgers

**Chinese specialty**

Preparation time: 1 hour

| |
|---|
| 2 tbs. dried Chinese mushrooms |
| 1 day-old roll |
| 5 green onions |
| ½ handful parsley |
| 1 egg |
| 1 tsp. curry powder |
| Pinch of ground coriander |
| Pinch of grated lemon rind |
| ½ tsp. salt |
| ⅔ lb. ground pork |
| 4 tbs. sesame seeds |
| 5 tbs. oil |
| 2 carrots |
| 2 tbs. soy sauce |
| 5 oz. canned soybean sprouts |
| 3 slices pineapple |
| 1 tbs. red wine vinegar |
| 1 tsp. cornstarch |
| 2 tbs. pineapple juice |
| Pinch of sugar |

Soak the mushrooms and bread in water. • Chop 2 green onions with the parsley and knead into the meat with the egg, spices, and the squeezed roll. • Make 8 patties and dredge them in the sesame seeds. • Preheat the oven to 250°. Sauté the burgers in the oil for 5 minutes on each side and keep warm in the oven. • Slice the onions into rings and slice the carrots. Put these and the mushrooms into the pan and sauté for 5 minutes. • Add the soy sauce, the drained sprouts, the diced pineapple and the vinegar and simmer gently for another 3 minutes. • Stir the starch into the pineapple juice, then add this to the vegetable mixture, thicken, and add salt and sugar to taste.

# Beef Steaks Tartare

### Famous recipe

Marinating time: 3 hours
Preparation time: 40 minutes

| 2 cloves of garlic |
| 2 shallots |
| 1¼ lb. ground round steak |
| ½ tsp. salt |
| ½ tsp. of dried sage |
| 2 pinches freshly ground white pepper |
| 2 tbs. tomato paste |
| 2 eggs |
| 6 tbs. bread crumbs |
| 3 tbs. coconut oil |

**P**eel and chop the garlic cloves and the shallots. •
Knead the ground meat with the garlic, shallots, salt, sage, pepper, tomato paste and the eggs. •
Make ½-inch thick patties of the ground meat about 2 inches wide, wrap them loosely in aluminum foil and marinate, refrigerated, for 3 hours. • Dredge the patties in the bread crumbs lightly on both sides. • Heat half of the oil and sauté half of the patties for 3 minutes on each side. Keep warm between two warm plates. Sauté the next batch of patties in fresh oil. •
Serve with French bread or toasted hamburger rolls, pickles, onion rings, sliced bell pepper, and Russian dressing or ketchup.

# Cevapcici with Onions

### Yugoslavian specialty, takes some time

Marinating time: 3 hours
Preparation time: 40 minutes

| ⅔ lb. ground beef |
| ⅔ lb. ground lamb |
| 3 cloves of garlic |
| 1 tsp. salt |
| ½ tsp. freshly ground white pepper |
| 3 large white onions |
| 4 tbs. olive oil |

**G**rind both meats in a meat grinder at the finest setting or knead together well. • Peel the garlic and crush into the meat, then add some salt and pepper and knead. • Make sausage-shaped rolls of the meat, about 3-inches long and 1-inch thick, then wrap the meat in aluminum foil and marinate in the refrigerator for 3 hours. •
Preheat the oven to 350°. • Peel and dice the onions and set aside, covered. • Heat the oil and sauté the meat rolls in it for about 10 minutes, until they are crispy brown. • Serve the cevapcici with the onions. • Fresh bread and tomato salad go well with this dish.

GREY Poupon
toothpaste
soap dish
A.1 & Barbecue sauce
Westexberry Sauce
Mayonne & Butter
Maple syrup egg
eggnoodles parsley
tomato sweet paste
carrots
broccoli
cream of mushrooms soup
pea pods
millet
dried curry coriander
white pepper

# Braised
# ishes

## Old French Veal Fricassee

### Famous recipe

Preparation time: 30 minutes
Cooking time: 1¼ hours

| |
|---|
| 1½ lb. veal shoulder |
| ½ lb. shallots |
| 1 onion |
| 1 carrot |
| 1 stalk celery |
| 5 sprigs parsley |
| 1 sprig fresh thyme |
| 1 bay leaf |
| 3 cloves |
| 2 tbs. butter |
| ½ tsp. salt |
| 2 pinches freshly ground white pepper |
| ½ cup dry white wine |
| ½ lb. mushrooms |
| 2 egg yolks |
| ½ cup cream |
| Juice of 1 lemon |
| Pinch of freshly grated nutmeg |
| 1 tsp. cornstarch |

Remove any membranes or fat from the meat, rinse and cut into 1½ inch pieces. • Peel the shallots, onion, and carrot. Rinse, trim and quarter the celery. • Rinse the parsley and thyme, then bind together with the carrot and celery. Stick the bay leaf and the cloves into the onion. • Sauté the meat and the shallots in the butter but do not brown. • Add the onion, vegetables, salt, pepper, wine and 2 cups water to the meat and simmer, covered, for 1 hour. • Remove the vegetables and onion from the fricassee, add the cleaned and halved mushrooms and simmer for another 15 minutes. • Whisk together the egg yolks, cream, lemon juice, nutmeg, and cornstarch, stir this into the fricassee and remove from heat. • Serve with egg noodles

## Stewed Veal Hocks

### Italian specialty

Preparation time: 30 minutes
Cooking time: 50 minutes

| | |
|---|---|
| 4 slices veal hocks (½ lb. each) | |
| 2 stalks of celery | |
| 1 large onion | |
| 2 carrots | |
| 1 tomato | |
| 3 tbs. flour | |
| 4 tbs. oil | |
| 1 tsp. each salt and freshly ground black pepper | |
| ½ cup dry white wine | |
| 1 tbs. tomato paste | |
| 2 tbs. chopped parsley | |
| 1 clove of garlic | |
| Grated rind of 1 lemon | |

**R**inse and dry the meat, then make incisions in the skin at the edge. • Rinse and trim the celery. Peel the onion and carrots. Chop all three. • Parboil the tomato, peel and dice. • Dredge the slices of meat in the flour and sauté briefly over high heat on both sides, then remove from heat and lightly salt and pepper. • Sauté the chopped vegetables in the grease briefly, add the meat and the tomato. Blend the wine with the tomato paste, pour it into the meat and allow the mixture to stew over low heat for 50 minutes. • Combine the parsley, chopped garlic and lemon rind. Stir this mixture into the sauce 10 minutes before the stewing is done. • A risotto with peas and Parmesan goes nicely with this dish.

## Shredded Veal Zurich Style

### Somewhat more expensive, quick

Preparation time: 30 minutes

| | |
|---|---|
| 1¼ lb. veal | |
| 1 large white onion | |
| 2 tbs. butter | |
| ½ tsp. each salt and freshly ground white pepper | |
| 1 tbs. flour | |
| ½ cup hot beef broth | |
| ½ tsp. white wine | |
| 3 tbs. crème fraîche | |

**R**inse and dry the meat, then slice it into ½-inch wide strips. • Peel and dice the onion. • Heat the butter and sauté the meat strips until light brown, then remove from heat. • Sauté the onions in the remaining grease until they are light brown, add the meat and salt and pepper. Sprinkle the flour over the meat, douse with the broth and wine and bring to a boil and turn off heat. • Remove the pan from the heat and add the crème fraîche. • Savory potato pancakes and a green salad go well with this.

Tip: The shredded meat can be spiced up with 1 teaspoon curry powder and 1 tablespoon capers.

## Veal Goulash with Whole-Grain Wheat

**Nutritious recipe**

Preparation time: 20 minutes
Cooking time: 1 hour

| |
|---|
| 1¼ lb. veal (boned breast) |
| 2 tbs. clarified butter |
| 1 bundle soup herbs (1 carrot, parsley root, piece of celeriac, piece of leek) |
| Rind of ½ lemon |
| Juice of 1 lemon |
| 2 pinches freshly ground white pepper |
| Pinch of cayenne pepper |
| ½ cup finely ground whole wheat |
| ¾ cup cream |
| 1 tsp. sea salt |
| 2 tbs. chopped parsley |

Rinse and dry the meat, then cut into 1-inch cubes. • Heat the clarified butter, sear the meat on all sides over high heat and remove from heat. • Trim, rinse and chop the soup herbs. • Cut the lemon rind into strips. • Add the vegetables, ½ cup water, the lemon juice, the lemon rind, the pepper and cayenne to the meat. Stew covered for 1 hour over low heat. • Blend the wheat with the cream, stir into the goulash and simmer gently for another 5 minutes. • Remove the goulash from the heat, remove the lemon rind and sprinkle the parsley over the stew. • Serve with mashed potatoes and a green salad.

## Shredded Veal with Almonds and Raisins

**Somewhat more expensive**

Preparation time: 50 minutes

| |
|---|
| 1½ lb. veal tenderloin |
| ¼ lb. raisins |
| 2 tbs. butter |
| 1 tbs. oil |
| ½ tsp. each salt and freshly ground white pepper |
| 4 shallots |
| ½ cup dry white wine |
| ¾ cup crème fraîche |
| 2 oz. slivered almonds |
| Pinch each ground cumin and coriander |
| 2 tbs. lemon juice |
| 2 sprigs peppermint |

Rinse and dry the meat, then cut it into ¼-inch strips. • Rinse the raisins in hot water and drain. • Heat the butter and oil, sear the meat over high heat turning it frequently, then lay it on a platter and salt and pepper. • Peel and chop the shallots, sauté them in the remaining fat until translucent, then douse with the white wine. Simmer and reduce the wine by half. • Whip the crème fraîche into the sauce and bring to a boil once again. • Add the raisins and almonds to the sauce and add salt, pepper, cumin, coriander, and lemon juice to taste. Allow the sauce to simmer gently another 10 minutes. • Add the shredded meat with its juices to the sauce, warm it and sprinkle peppermint over it. • Serve with buttered rice.

## Lamb Ragout with Rye

**Nutritious**

Preparation time: 45 minutes

| | |
|---|---|
| ¾ lb. lamb | |
| 2 onions | |
| 2 garlic cloves | |
| 4 tbs. olive oil | |
| ¼ tsp. freshly ground black pepper | |
| ⅛ tsp. cayenne pepper | |
| ¼ cup coarsely ground rye | |
| 1 tsp. sea salt | |
| 1 cup dry red wine | |
| ½ cup cream | |
| 3 tbs. chopped chives | |

Rinse the meat, dry and cut into 1-inch cubes. • Cube the onions and garlic and sauté in the hot oil until translucent. Remove with a slotted spoon and place to the side. • Add the meat to the hot oil and sprinkle with a little pepper. Sear well on all sides over high heat, about 5 minutes. • Sprinkle the cayenne pepper, the rye and the salt over the meat and sauté, stirring frequently, an additional 2 minutes. • Add the onions and garlic, the wine and 1 cup water. Simmer in an open pot until the meat is tender. • Remove the ragout from the heat and mix in the cream and chives.

## Lamb Ragout with White Beans

**Requires some time**

Soaking time: 12 hours
Preparation time: 40 minutes
Cooking time: 1 hour

| | |
|---|---|
| ¾ cup white beans | |
| 1 bunch soup herbs | |
| 1¾ lbs. lamb shoulder | |
| 3 tbs. olive oil | |
| 3 cups tomatoes | |
| 1¾ cups onions | |
| 1 tsp. each salt and freshly ground black pepper | |
| 1 sprig fresh rosemary | |
| 1 bay leaf | |
| 1 clove | |
| 1 cup beef broth | |
| 2 tbs. vinegar | |
| 2 tbs. chopped parsley | |

Soak the beans 12 hours in cold water. • Rinse the soup herbs, trim and cut into pieces. Cook with the beans in the soaking water until almost done, about 45 minutes. • Rinse the meat, dry and cut into 1-inch cubes. Brown by portions in hot oil and place to the side. • Skin and coarsely chop the tomatoes. • Peel the onions and sauté until translucent in the remaining oil. Add the tomatoes, the meat and the spices, then pour in the beef broth. Cook covered over medium heat 1 hour. • Add the beans 20 minutes before the end of the cooking time. Season the ragout with the vinegar and sprinkle with parsley. • Good with fresh white bread.

## Lamb Stew with Zucchini

**Requires some time**

Preparation time: 1 hour

| 1¼ lbs. lamb |
| --- |
| 1 tbs. cornstarch |
| 1 tsp. freshly ground black pepper |
| ½ tsp. dried oregano |
| 1 onion |
| 3 garlic cloves |
| 1 lb. zucchini |
| 2 tbs. butter |
| 1 tbs. oil |
| 1 cup beef broth |
| ½ cup dry red wine |

**R**inse the meat, dry, slice into strips ¼-inch thick and rub with the cornstarch, pepper and oregano. • Finely chop the onion. Cut the garlic cloves into slivers. Wash the zucchini and cut into ½-inch thick slices. • Heat the butter and the oil, then brown the meat in portions and place it to the side. • Sauté the onion and garlic in the oil until translucent. Add the zucchini and heat briefly. Add the beef broth and the wine, bring to a boil, then add the meat together with any juices and heat. • Serve with rice.

## Lamb Pilaf

**Requires some time**

Preparation time: 20 minutes
Cooking time: 50 minutes
Serves: 6 people

| 2 lbs. lamb |
| --- |
| 4 onions |
| 2 garlic cloves |
| 1 lb. tomatoes |
| 5 tbs. olive oil |
| 1 tbs. sweet paprika |
| 1 tsp. each salt and freshly ground black pepper |
| ⅛ tsp. sugar |
| ½ cup dry red wine |
| ½ lb. cabbage |
| 2 cups beef broth |
| 1½ cups long-grain rice |
| 1 tbs. lemon juice |
| Pinch freshly ground nutmeg |
| 2 tbs. chopped parsley |

**R**inse the meat, dry and cut into 1-inch cubes. • Peel and dice the onions and the garlic cloves. • Skin the tomatoes and dice. • Heat the oil and brown the meat. Add the onions and garlic and sauté until the meat is brown and the onions are translucent. • Add the tomatoes, the spices and the red wine. Cover and let the meat stew for 20 minutes. • Trim the cabbage and cut into strips. • Mix the beef broth, the cabbage and the rice into the meat and cook over medium heat for an additional 20 minutes. • Season with the lemon juice and nutmeg and sprinkle with parsley.

## Aromatic and Spicy Venison Ragout

### Requires some time

Preparation time: 40 minutes
Marinating time: 24 hours
Cooking time: 1½ hours

| | |
|---|---|
| 2 lbs. venison (for ragout) | |
| 1 lemon | |
| 2 onions | |
| 2 bay leaves | |
| 6 cloves | |
| 1 2-inch piece of leek | |
| 1 carrot | |
| 6 tbs. oil | |
| 5 black peppercorns | |
| 3 tbs. wine vinegar | |
| 2 cups Burgundy wine | |
| 1 tsp. salt | |
| ½ tsp. freshly ground black pepper | |
| ½ cup beef broth | |
| 2 tbs. flour | |
| 1 tsp. sugar | |
| 1 tbs. cranberry jelly | |

**R**inse the meat. • Cut a thick slice out of the lemon. Peel an onion and stud it with one bay leaf and 3 cloves. • Clean the vegetables, dice and sauté for 5 minutes in 1 tablespoon of oil. • Marinate the meat with the studded onion, the vegetables, the lemon slice, the peppercorns, the vinegar and the wine (reserving 4 tablespoons) for 24 hours, covered, in a cool place. Turn frequently. • Dab the meat dry, brown for 15 minutes in 3 tablespoons of oil, salt and pepper. • Strain the marinade and stew the meat in it for 1 hour. • Remove the bones and cube the meat. • Heat the beef broth. Measure ½ cup of the stewing liquid. • Heat the remaining oil and brown the flour and sugar in it until golden. Add the beef broth, the reserved stewing liquid and the second studded onion. Then add the meat and stew 15 minutes. • Remove the onion. Season the ragout with the jelly, the remaining red wine and a little vinegar. • Serve with egg noodles.

## Oxtail Ragout

**Nutritious, takes some time**

Preparation time: 30 minutes
Cooking time: 2½ hours

| |
|---|
| 2½ lbs. oxtail, in 2-inch pieces |
| 1 lb. onions |
| 2 garlic cloves |
| ½ cup carrots |
| ½ cup celery root |
| 4 tbs. olive oil |
| 2 cups dry red wine |
| ½ tsp. each caraway and dried thyme |
| 2 bay leaves |
| ¼ tsp. freshly ground black pepper |
| 1 tbs. granulated vegetable bouillon |
| ¼ cup rye flour |
| ½ cup cream |
| 2 tbs. chopped parsley |

**R**inse and dry the meat. • Chop the onions and the garlic cloves. Wash and peel the carrots, then dice the carrots and the celery root. • Heat the oil and sear the meat over a high heat. Add the vegetables and continue sautéing until the onions are translucent. • Add the wine and the spices. Cover and stew until tender, approximately 2 hours. • Remove the bones. • Mix the rye flour with the cream and a little water until smooth. • Strain the stewing liquid, bring to a boil and add the flour mixture while stirring. Simmer gently for 5 minutes. • Heat the meat in the sauce. Taste the ragout for seasoning and sprinkle with the parsley. • Delicious served with broccoli.

# Rump Roast with Apple-Horseradish and Chive Sauce

## Austrian specialty, takes some time

Preparation time: 2½ hours
Serves: 8 people

| |
|---|
| 2 lbs. beef rump roast |
| 2 beef marrow bones |
| 2 tsp. salt |
| 1 onion |
| 1 medium carrot |
| 1 cup celery root |
| 1 bay leaf |
| 3 cloves |
| 1 tsp. black peppercorns |
| For the apple-horseradish: |
| ½ horseradish root |
| 2 tbs. white wine vinegar |
| 2 medium, tart apples |
| 1 tbs. sugar |
| 2 pinches salt |

| |
|---|
| For the chive sauce: |
| 1 day-old roll |
| 5 tbs. milk |
| 2 hard-boiled egg yolks |
| 2 tbs. oil |
| 1 tsp. sugar |
| 2 tbs. white wine vinegar |
| ⅛ tsp. each salt and freshly ground white pepper |
| 4 tbs. chopped chives |

**R**inse the roast and the bones. • Bring to a boil approximately 3 quarts of water with the salt. Add the roast and the bones and boil gently in an open pot for 30 minutes. Skim any foam that collects. • Regulate the heat so that the water barely simmers. Place a lid on the pot, but leave an opening. • Peel the onion, the carrot and the celery. Stud the onion with the bay leaf and the cloves.

• After 1½ hours of cooking, add the vegetables and peppercorns to the meat. Cook an additional hour. • For the apple-horseradish, peel, wash and grate the horseradish. Mix with the vinegar, cover, and place to the side. • Wash, peel, quarter and core the apples. Steam them covered for ten minutes with the sugar and 1 tablespoon of water. • Press the apple quarters through a very fine sieve, mix them with the horseradish and season to taste with salt. • For the chive sauce, grate the crust from the roll and soften the roll in the milk. • Puree the milk-soaked roll with the egg yolks. Season the puree with the oil, sugar, vinegar, salt and pepper and mix with the chives. • Carve the roast, arrange on a warm platter and sprinkle with a little hot broth. • Slice the vegetables and garnish the meat. • Serve

the remaining broth with an already-prepared addition as a first-course soup. (Cover the roast with a double layer of aluminum foil and keep warm in a 350° oven.) • Serve the meat with the apple-horseradish and the chive sauce. • Excellent with home-fried potatoes and creamed spinach.

## Beef Stroganoff

**Famous recipe, slightly expensive**

Preparation time: 40 minutes

| |
|---|
| 1 medium onion |
| ½ lb. small mushrooms |
| 1¼ lbs. sirloin tips |
| 3 tbs. clarified butter |
| 1 tsp. sweet paprika |
| ½ tsp. salt |
| ½ cup dry white wine |
| ½ cup beef broth |
| ⅔ cup crème fraîche |
| 1 tbs. butter |
| 1 medium pickle |
| ½ tsp. mildly spicy mustard |
| 1 bunch of chives |

Finely chop the onion. Clean the mushrooms and slice. • Remove any skin from the meat, wash, dry and cut into 1-inch cubes. • Heat the clarified butter and brown the meat and chopped onion. Season with the paprika and salt. Brown the meat an additional 2 minutes over medium heat. Remove from the pan and keep warm in aluminum foil. • Add the white wine to the pan, then add the mushrooms and reduce the liquid by half while stirring. Add the beef broth, bring to a boil and stir in the crème fraîche and the butter. • Chop the pickle. Add it and the meat to the sauce and warm, then season the dish with the mustard. • Chop the chives and sprinkle over the meat. • Serve with egg noodles.

## Sirloin Tips in Tarragon Cream

**Slightly expensive, fast**

Preparation time: 30 minutes

| |
|---|
| 1¼ lbs. sirloin tips |
| 1 shallot or small onion |
| 2 tbs. clarified butter |
| ½ cup dry white wine |
| 1 cup cream |
| 1 bunch tarragon |
| ¼ tsp. grated horseradish |
| ¼ tsp. salt |
| ⅛ tsp. freshly ground white pepper |
| 1 pinch sugar |
| 2 egg yolks |

Rinse the meat, dry and cut into thin slices (approximately ¼-inch thick). • Finely chop the shallot. • Heat the clarified butter and sear the meat in portions, removing each portion and placing it to the side. • Sauté the shallot in the remaining butter until golden; then add the wine and cream and stir until thick. • Wash the tarragon, spin dry and finely chop. • Season the cream sauce with the horseradish, salt, pepper and sugar. Blend the egg yolks with a little of the hot sauce. Remove the remaining sauce from the heat and thicken with the egg yolk mixture. • Warm the sirloin tips in the sauce and serve sprinkled with the tarragon. • Good accompanied by wild rice and early peas.

## Budapest Goulash

### Hungarian specialty

Preparation time: 15 minutes
Cooking time: 1 hour

| | |
|---|---|
| 1¾ lbs. beef | |
| 2¼ cups onions | |
| 2 garlic cloves | |
| 3-4 slices bacon | |
| 2 tbs. bacon fat | |
| ⅛ tsp. salt | |
| 3 tbs. sweet paprika | |
| 1 tsp. hot paprika | |
| ½ tsp. each ground caraway and dried marjoram | |
| 2 tbs. tomato paste | |
| 1 cup beef broth | |
| ½ lb. boiling potatoes | |
| 1 green and 1 red pepper | |

**R**inse the meat, dry and cut into 1-inch cubes. • Peel and finely chop the onions and the garlic cloves. • Cut the bacon into small pieces and brown in the fat. Add the onions and garlic and sauté until translucent. • Add the meat and brown over high heat until it is gray. • Stir in the spices, the tomato paste and ½ cup beef broth. Reduce heat to medium, cover and stew 30 minutes. • Peel the potatoes and cut into cubes. Wash and trim the peppers, then cut into pieces. • Add the potatoes to the goulash with the remaining beef broth and cook for 15 minutes. • Add the peppers and cook an additional fifteen minutes.

## Hungarian Goulash

### Requires some time

Preparation time: 40 minutes
Cooking time: 1¼ hours
Serves: 8 people

| | |
|---|---|
| 2 lbs. beef neck | |
| 1½ cups onions | |
| 1 cup carrots | |
| ¾ cup white turnips | |
| ¾ cup celery root | |
| 3 tbs. bacon fat | |
| 3 tbs. sweet paprika | |
| 1 tsp. hot paprika | |
| 1 cup hot beef broth | |
| 1¾ lbs. boiling potatoes | |
| 1 tsp. caraway | |
| ½ tsp. salt | |

**R**inse the meat, dry and cut into 1-inch cubes. • Chop the onions. Wash and peel the carrots, the turnips and the celery. Cut the carrots in slivers, the turnips in thin slices and the celery in cubes. • Heat the fat. Sauté the onion until translucent, then add and brown the meat. Sprinkle the paprika over the meat and mix in the prepared vegetables. Add the beef broth, cover and simmer gently for 45 minutes. • Wash and peel the potatoes, then cube (not too small). Add to the meat with the caraway and salt. Cook an additional 30 minutes.

## Beef with Vegetables

**Takes some time**

Preparation time: 30 minutes
Cooking time: 1½ hours
Serves: 6 people

| | |
|---|---|
| 2 lbs. beef roast | |
| 1 tsp. salt | |
| ½ tsp. freshly ground black pepper | |
| 2 tbs. white wine vinegar | |
| 1 bay leaf | |
| 1 clove | |
| 1 tsp. each whole allspice and coriander | |
| 1 cup shallots | |
| 1¼ cups carrots | |
| 1 kohlrabi | |
| 2 leeks | |
| 2 tomatoes | |
| ½ cup crème fraîche | |
| 2 tbs. chopped parsley | |
| ½ tsp. herb salt | |

Rinse the meat and rub with the salt and pepper. • Bring 1 cup of water with the vinegar to a boil in a steamer. • Place the meat with the spices in the steamer, cover tightly and steam for 1 hour. • Peel or trim the vegetables, wash and cut into pieces of roughly the same size. Skin and quarter the tomatoes. • Remove the spices from the steamer. Add the shallots, the carrots and the kohlrabi to the meat and steam for 20 minutes. • Then add the leeks and the tomatoes and steam for an additional 10 minutes. • Carve the meat and keep warm. • Reduce the cooking liquid by half. Blend in the crème fraîche, the parsley and the herb salt. Serve with the meat. • Potatoes are a good accompaniment.

## Ragout of Beef Heart

**Inexpensive, requires some time**

Preparation time: 30 minutes
Cooking time: 1½ hours

| | |
|---|---|
| 1½ lbs. beef heart | |
| 2 tbs. flour | |
| 1 large onion | |
| ¾ cup leek | |
| 2 tbs. clarified butter | |
| 2 tsp. tomato paste | |
| ¼ tsp. each salt and freshly ground white pepper | |
| ¼ tsp. hot paprika | |
| 1 cup beef broth | |
| ½ cup sour cream | |
| 2 egg yolks | |
| 2 tbs. chopped chives | |

Rinse the heart, being careful to wash out any remaining blood. Remove any hard blood vessels, tendons and fat. Cut the heart into 1½ inch cubes and dredge in the flour. • Peel and dice the onion. Wash and trim the leek, then cut into slices. • Heat the clarified butter and brown the onion and leek until the onion is translucent. Add the meat and brown over medium heat for 5 minutes. • Mix the tomato paste and the spices into the beef broth. Add half of the liquid to the meat. Cover the meat and stew for 1½ hours over low heat. Add the remaining beef broth during the cooking time and, if necessary, a little water. • Blend the sour cream with the egg yolks. Remove the ragout from the heat, thicken with the egg yolk mixture and sprinkle with chives. • Serve with mashed potatoes and pickled beets.

# Beef à la Mode

**Famous recipe, requires some time**

Preparation time: 30 minutes
Marinating time: 8 hours
Cooking time: 2 hours
Serves: 10 people

| |
|---|
| 4½ lbs. beef rump roast |
| 4 slices bacon |
| ½ tsp. coarsely ground black pepper |
| 1 bay leaf |
| Pinch of freshly ground nutmeg |
| 1 tsp. dried thyme |
| 2 cups dry red wine |
| ½ cup cognac or brandy |
| 2 onions |
| 2 carrots |
| 1 cup celery root |
| 4 tbs. oil |
| 1 heaping tsp. flour |
| 1 tbs. tomato paste |
| 1 tsp. salt |

**R**inse the meat and dry. • Cube the bacon and mix it with the meat, the spices, the wine and the cognac in a bowl. • Peel, wash and dice the vegetables. Add to the meat and marinate covered for 8 hours. • Preheat the oven to 300°. • Pour the meat with the vegetables into a sieve. Reserve the liquid. • Heat the oil and sear the meat on all sides, then remove. Brown the vegetables and the bacon for 3 minutes in the oil. Sprinkle in the flour, brown until golden, then mix in the tomato paste. Add the marinating liquid and the meat to the pot, sprinkle with salt and cook covered for 2 hours in the oven. • Turn the meat 4 times and add some red wine if necessary. • Carve the roast and keep warm. Pour the sauce through a very fine sieve. • Good with noodles and savoy cabbage.

## Beef Roulades with Bacon Stuffing

**Requires some time**

Preparation time: 30 minutes
Cooking time: 1 hour

| |
|---|
| 4 beef roulades (¼ lb. each) |
| 1 tbs. mildly spicy mustard |
| 1 onion |
| 1 garlic clove |
| 2 leeks |
| 2 carrots |
| 4 slices bacon |
| 2 tsp. curry powder |
| 2 tbs. coconut oil |
| 1 tsp. each salt and freshly ground pepper |
| ½ cup hot beef broth |
| ½ cup dry red wine |
| 2 tsp. flour |

Spread the roulades with the mustard. Chop the onion and the garlic and sprinkle on the roulades. • Wash the white part of the leeks and cut into strips. Peel and wash the carrots and cut into strips with the bacon. • Spread the vegetable and bacon strips over the roulades and sprinkle with the curry. • Roll the roulades, tie with string and brown in the oil over a high heat. Salt and pepper the meat, then add the beef broth and the wine. Cover and stew for 1 hour over low heat. • Blend the flour with a little water. • Arrange the roulades on a serving dish, remove the string. Bind the sauce with the flour mixture, simmer for 5 minutes and serve separately. • Good accompanied by mashed potatoes.

## Roulades with Mushroom Stuffing

**Requires some time**

Preparation time: 45 minutes
Cooking time: 50 minutes

| |
|---|
| 2 tbs. dried mushrooms |
| 5 slices bacon |
| 2 small onions |
| 1 tsp. dried thyme |
| 2 tbs. bread crumbs |
| 8 beef roulades (2 oz. each) |
| 1 tsp. each salt and freshly ground black pepper |
| 2 tbs. clarified butter |
| 1 cup dry red wine |
| 5 tbs. crème fraîche |
| 2 tbs. chopped parsley |

Soak the mushrooms for 25 minutes in warm water. • Fry the bacon until crisp. Sauté the chopped onion in the bacon fat until translucent. • Chop the drained mushrooms. Sauté them for 10 minutes with the onion, then mix with the thyme and bread crumbs. • Rub the roulades with salt and pepper, spread with the mushroom mixture, roll and tie with string. • Heat the butter and sear the roulades. Add the red wine and cook covered for 50 minutes over low heat. • After 25 minutes mix the crème fraîche and the strained mushroom water into the stewing liquid. • Serve the roulades in the sauce with the parsley.

## Veal Roulades with Mushroom Stuffing

**Slightly expensive**

Preparation time: 35 minutes
Cooking time: 45 minutes

| |
|---|
| 4 veal cutlets (¼ lb. each) |
| 5 slices of bacon |
| 2 onions |
| 1 lb. mushrooms |
| 8 sage leaves |
| 2 tbs. oil |
| ⅛ tsp. salt |
| ½ tsp. freshly ground white pepper |
| 1 cup chicken broth |
| ½ cup dry white wine |
| 3 tbs. crème fraîche |
| 1 tsp. cornstarch |
| Pinch of hot paprika |

**R**inse the cutlets and dry. • Chop the bacon and the onions. Clean the mushrooms and thinly slice half of them. • Fry the bacon, then sauté half of the onions until translucent. Add the mushroom slices and sauté 5 minutes. Spread the mixture on the roulades, place 2 sage leaves on each, roll up and tie with string. • Heat the oil and sauté the remaining onions until translucent. Sear the roulades until brown. Season with the salt and pepper, then add the broth and wine. Cover and stew for 30 minutes. • Halve the remaining mushrooms, add to the roulades and cook an additional 10 minutes. • Blend the crème fraîche with the cornstarch and paprika, then blend the mixture into the sauce. Bring to a boil and remove from the heat. • Serve the roulades in the sauce with egg noodles and grilled tomatoes.

## Pork Roulades with Cheese Stuffing

**Slightly expensive**

Preparation time: 1 hour

| |
|---|
| 4 pork cutlets (¼ lb. each) |
| 1 bunch of basil |
| ½ tsp. each salt and freshly ground white pepper |
| 1 tsp. lemon juice |
| ½ cup cream cheese |
| 1 lb. tomatoes |
| ½ lb. mozzarella |
| 2 garlic cloves |
| 4 thin slices of Parma ham (about 2 oz.) |
| 3 tbs. olive oil |
| 1 cup hot beef broth |
| 1 tbs. tomato paste |
| 1 tsp. cornstarch |

**R**inse the cutlets and dry. • Chop the basil and mix into the cream cheese with 1 pinch each of salt and pepper and with the lemon juice. • Skin the tomatoes and cut into strips. Dice the mozzarella. Cut the garlic into thin slices. • Spread the cutlets with the cream cheese and place 1 slice of ham on top of each cutlet. Distribute the tomato strips, the diced cheese and the garlic slices over the cutlets, roll them up, tie with string and rub with the remaining salt and pepper. • Heat the oil, sear the roulades until brown, add the broth and stew covered for 45 minutes. • Remove the string and keep the roulades warm. • Reduce the sauce slightly. Blend the tomato paste with the cornstarch, then thicken the sauce with it. Pour over the roulades.

## Pork Tenderloin with Yogurt Sauce

### Slightly difficult

Preparation time: 30 minutes
Cooking time: 40 minutes

| |
| --- |
| 2 pork tenderloins (14 oz. each) |
| ¼ cup Emmenthaler cheese |
| 1 onion |
| ½ tsp. salt |
| ⅛ tsp. freshly ground white pepper |
| 1 tbs. flour |
| 2 tbs. coconut oil |
| ⅔ cup yogurt |
| 2 tbs. granulated bouillon |
| 1 tbs. sweet paprika |
| 1 tbs. chopped basil |

Rinse the tenderloins, dry and remove any skin or fat. • Cut the cheese into thin slivers (about 1½ inches long and ⅓ inch wide). • Peel and chop the onion. • Rub the meat with the salt and pepper. Pierce small holes into the meat at regular intervals with a sharp knife. • Insert the cheese slivers into the holes so that they protrude slightly. • Dredge the tenderloins in the flour. • Heat the oil and sear the tenderloins on all sides until brown; this takes about ten minutes. The protruding cheese slivers should melt. • After five minutes add the chopped onion and sauté until translucent. • Blend the yogurt with the granulated bouillon and paprika, then add to the tenderloins. Cover and stew over low heat for 40 minutes. Baste the meat frequently with the yogurt sauce. • Arrange the tenderloins for serving by pouring the sauce over them and sprinkling with the basil. • Serve with boiled potatoes and glazed carrots.

## Roast Veal

**Requires some time, slightly expensive**

Preparation time: 30 minutes
Marinating time: 24 hours
Cooking time: 1¾ hours

| |
|---|
| 2 lbs. veal roast |
| ½ tsp. freshly ground white pepper |
| 4 shallots |
| 2 garlic cloves |
| 2 sprigs each fresh rosemary and thyme |
| ½ bay leaf |
| 1 cup dry, aromatic white wine |
| 4 tbs. oil |
| ½ tsp. salt |
| ½ cup hot beef broth |
| 1 tsp. fresh rosemary, chopped |
| 5 tbs. crème fraîche |

**R**inse the meat, dry and rub with the pepper. • Peel and chop the shallots and the garlic. • Wash the herbs, spin dry and chop. Mix them with the shallots, the garlic, the bay leaf, the white wine (reserving 2 tablespoons) and 1 tablespoon of oil. • Place the meat in a plastic bag that is not too large, pour in the marinade and close. Massage the marinade in the bag into the meat. • Marinate the meat for 24 hours in the refrigerator. During this time repeatedly massage the marinade into the meat. • Pour the marinade into a bowl. Dab the meat dry and rub with the salt on all sides. • Strain the marinade. • Heat the remaining oil in a large roasting pan and sear the meat over a high heat on all sides until brown, approximately 15 minutes. • Remove the meat

from the pot. Add half the marinade and stir with a spoon to scrape any drippings from the bottom of the pan. Part of the liquid may steam away. • Bring the remaining marinade to a boil, add the meat, then gradually add the boiling hot beef broth. • Cover and stew the meat for 30 minutes over medium heat, then for 1 hour over low heat. The liquid should not boil, but rather gently simmer. Baste the meat with the liquid every 15 minutes. • Preheat the oven to 400°. Have a large piece of doubled aluminum foil ready. • Wrap the done meat in the foil and keep warm in the oven. • Strain the cooking liquid and blend with the remaining white wine, the rosemary and the crème fraîche. If necessary, season the sauce

with salt and pepper. • Slice the roast, arrange on a warm platter and pour some of the sauce over it. Serve the remaining sauce separately. • Serve with potato croquettes and salad or broccoli.

## Szegeny Goulash

**Famous recipe, inexpensive**

Preparation time: 25 minutes
Cooking time: 45 minutes

| |
|---|
| 1¼ lbs. pork belly |
| 4 onions |
| 1 garlic clove |
| 2 tbs. shortening |
| 2 cups hot beef broth |
| 1-2 tsp. hot paprika |
| 2 cups sauerkraut |
| 1 tbs. flour |
| 1 cup sour cream |
| ½ tsp. each salt and freshly ground white pepper |

**R**inse the pork belly and dab dry. Cut the meat into 1-inch cubes. • Peel and chop the onions and garlic. • Heat the shortening and sear the meat while turning. Add the onion and garlic and sauté until translucent. • Add about ½ cup beef broth and allow the liquid to steam off. • Sprinkle the paprika over the meat, then add the sauerkraut and remaining beef broth. Mix well, cover and stew over low heat for 40 minutes. • Blend the flour with the sour cream and thicken the goulash with it. Simmer 5 minutes. • Season with salt and pepper before serving. • Good with bread dumplings and field or chicory salad.

## Paprika Goulash

**Requires some time**

Preparation time: 30 minutes
Cooking time: 1 hour
Serves: 6 people

| |
|---|
| 2 lbs. beef brisket |
| 2 cups onions |
| 2 garlic cloves |
| 2 cups tomatoes |
| 3 tbs. oil |
| 1½ tbs. flour |
| 3 tsp. sweet paprika |
| 1 tsp. hot paprika |
| 1 cup hot chicken broth |
| 2 red bell peppers |
| ½ tsp. salt |

**R**inse the meat, dry and cut into 1-inch cubes. • Peel and chop the onions and garlic. • Skin and quarter the tomatoes. • Heat the oil and sauté the onion and garlic until translucent. Add the meat and turn until gray over a high heat. • Mix the flour with the paprika and sprinkle over the meat. Brown briefly, then add the hot chicken broth. Add the tomatoes, cover and cook over a low heat for 50 minutes. • Wash, dry, and halve the bell peppers. Remove the seeds and membranes, then chop. Add them to the goulash after 50 minutes cooking time and cook an additional 10 minutes. • Season with salt before serving. • Good with egg noodles.

## Sweet-and-Sour Pork

**An Indo-Chinese speciality**

Preparation time: 45 minutes

| |
|---|
| 1 lb. pork cutlet |
| 1 tbs. soy sauce |
| 4 green onions |
| 2 garlic cloves |
| 1 green bell pepper |
| 3 medium tomatoes |
| 2 slices fresh pineapple |
| 1 cup mushrooms |
| 1 tbs. arrowroot |
| 4 tbs. oil |
| ½ tsp. salt |
| ⅛ tsp. cayenne pepper |
| 1 tbs. sugar |
| 2 tbs. vinegar |
| 2 tbs. pineapple juice |
| 1 tbs. rice wine or sherry |

**R**inse the meat, dry and slice into strips. Sprinkle with the soy sauce, cover and marinate. • Wash and trim the onions and cut into rings. Chop the garlic. Wash and chop the bell pepper. Skin the tomatoes and cut into pieces. • Peel the pineapple slices, core and cut into small pieces. Clean the mushrooms and slice. • Dredge the meat strips in the arrowroot and sauté until brown in the heated oil. Season with salt and cayenne pepper and keep warm. • Sauté the onion with the garlic and mushrooms over high heat in the oil for 1 minute. Add the vegetables and pineapple and sauté an additional 2 minutes. • Mix the sugar, vinegar, pineapple juice and rice wine into the vegetables and bring to a boil. • Pour the vegetables over the meat.

## Chinese Stir-Fried Pork

**Inexpensive, easy to prepare**

Preparation time: 40 minutes

| |
|---|
| 1 pork cutlet (14 oz.) |
| 2 bamboo shoots (canned) |
| 2 medium carrots |
| ⅔ cup savoy cabbage |
| 2 green onions |
| 6 tbs. fresh soy sprouts |
| 3 tbs. oil |
| 2 tbs. soy sauce |
| ⅛ tsp. each salt and freshly ground white pepper |
| ½ tsp. cornstarch |

**R**inse and dry the meat, remove any fat or skin and cut into thin strips. • Cut the bamboo shoots into ½-inch strips. Wash and peel the carrots and cut them into fine slivers. Wash and trim the cabbage and cut into strips. Wash and trim the onions and cut into rings. • Rinse and drain the soy sprouts. • Heat half of the oil in a large pan. Brown the meat in portions and place to the side. • Add the remaining oil to the pan and sauté the vegetables in the order of preparation. Do not overcook the vegetables. Add the meat and season with the soy sauce, salt and pepper. Heat well. • Blend the cornstarch with 2 tablespoons water and thicken the sauce with the mixture. • Serve with rice.

Tip: Placing the meat in the freezer for 30 minutes before slicing makes it easier to cut evenly.

## Meatballs with Whole-Wheat Bread

**Nutritious**

Preparation time: 40 minutes
Cooking time: 25 minutes

1 cup milk
4 slices whole-wheat bread
1 lb. lean ground veal
2 onions
1 small bunch soup herbs
1 egg
1 tsp. sea salt
½ tsp. each freshly ground white pepper and paprika
Pinch cayenne pepper
2 tsp. granulated vegetable bouillon
¼ cup whole-wheat flour
½ cup cream
Juice of ½ lemon
1 tbs. finely chopped parsley

Bring the milk to a boil. Cut the bread into pieces and soak in the hot milk. • Clean and chop the onions and herbs. Mix with the meat. • Press the liquid out of the bread and mix with the egg, the salt, some pepper, the paprika and cayenne pepper. Knead with the meat. • Boil 2 cups of water with the granulated bouillon. With wet hands shape 12 meatballs and cook for 20 minutes in the bouillon. • Blend the flour with the cream and the remaining milk. • Drain the meatballs and keep warm. • Stir the flour mixture into the broth and continue stirring while simmering for 5 minutes. • Season the sauce with the remaining pepper and the lemon juice. Pour over the meatballs and sprinkle with parsley. • Serve with Risi-Pisi (rice with peas).

## Meatballs with Millet

**Nutritious**

Preparation time: 1 hour

1 large onion
¼ cup butter
½ cup millet flour
1 tsp. sea salt
9 oz. ground sirloin
⅛ tsp. freshly ground black pepper
1 tsp. chopped basil
½ tsp. ground coriander
Pinch of cayenne pepper
1 egg
2 tbs. each finely chopped parsley and chives
4 tbs. cream

Peel and chop the onions and sauté until translucent in the melted butter. Add the millet and stir for 2 minutes before mixing in 1½ cups water and a little salt. Cover and cook over low heat for 15 minutes. Turn off the heat and let the millet soak for an additional 15 minutes. • Mix half of the millet with a little salt, the ground meat, the spices, the egg and 1 tablespoon of each of the herbs. • Bring the remaining millet and salt to a boil in 1½ cups water. • Shape 12 meatballs and cook for 15 minutes in the millet broth; turn them after 8 minutes. • Stir the remaining herbs and the cream into the sauce. • Serve with salad.

## Meatballs in Caper Sauce

**Inexpensive, easy to prepare**

Preparation time: 45 minutes

| |
|---|
| 2 anchovy fillets |
| 10 pitted green olives |
| 1 egg |
| 3 tbs. bread crumbs |
| 1 lb. ground beef |
| 1 onion |
| 1 tsp. each salt and freshly ground black pepper |
| ½ tsp. grated lemon rind |
| Pinch of freshly ground nutmeg |
| 1 qt. beef broth |
| 3 tbs. butter |
| ¼ cup flour |
| 1 cup hot milk |
| 3 tbs. small capers |
| 1 tbs. lemon juice |
| 4 tbs. cream |
| 1 egg yolk |

Finely chop the anchovies and olives and mix into the ground meat with the egg and the bread crumbs. • Peel the onion and grate into the mixture. Work in ½ teaspoon each salt and pepper, the lemon rind and the nutmeg. • Shape walnut-size meatballs from the meat. • Bring the beef broth to a boil. Cook the meatballs in the broth over low heat for 10 minutes, drain and keep warm. • Melt the butter, sprinkle the flour in and brown until golden. Gradually add the milk and then 2 cups of the broth. Simmer the sauce gently for 5 minutes. Stir the capers into the sauce with the remaining broth, the lemon juice, and the remaining salt and pepper. • Blend the cream with the egg yolk and thicken the sauce with it. Place the meatballs in the sauce and heat, but do not allow to boil. • Serve with potatoes in their jackets.

## Veal Sweetbreads in Mushroom Cream Sauce

### Requires some time, slightly difficult

Soaking time: 2 hours
Preparation time: 1 hour

| | |
|---|---|
| 1¼ lbs. calf sweetbreads | |
| 2 tbs. vinegar | |
| 1½ tsp. salt | |
| 1 cup small mushrooms | |
| ½ bunch parsley | |
| 2 tbs. butter | |
| 1 cup hot beef broth | |
| 1 tsp. dried rosemary | |
| 1 tbs. cornstarch | |

S oak the sweetbreads until all traces of blood have disappeared. Change the water frequently. • Rinse the sweetbreads and place in a pot with 2 quarts of water, the vinegar and 1 teaspoon salt. Bring to a boil and cook gently over low heat for 15 minutes. • Plunge the sweetbreads into cold water, strip off the skin and remove any gristle and bloody spots. Cut the sweetbreads into slices. • Clean and slice the mushrooms. Wash, spin dry and chop the parsely. Cover and place to the side. • Melt the butter in a large pan over a low heat and lightly brown the sweetbread slices on both sides. Gradually add the beef broth, then the mushrooms and the rosemary. Cover and cook an additional 15 minutes. • Blend the cornstarch with a little cold water and thicken the sauce with it. Bring just to a boil, then season with salt and sprinkle with parsley. • Serve with egg noodles and carrot salad.

## Sour Liver

### Famous recipe, fast

Preparation time: 30 minutes

| | |
|---|---|
| 1¼ lbs. calf liver | |
| 2 tbs. each butter and flour | |
| 1 cup hot beef broth | |
| ½ cup milk | |
| 1 tbs. lemon juice | |
| 1 tbs. white wine vinegar | |
| ½ bay leaf | |
| ¼ tsp. freshly ground white pepper | |
| ½ tsp. salt | |
| 5 tbs. crème fraîche | |

R inse the liver, dry and remove any bits of skin or blood vessels. Cut the liver into slices ½-inch thick. • Melt the butter in a large pan, sprinkle the flour in and brown until golden. Stir the beef broth into the roux until smoothly blended with the butter and flour. Add the remaining beef broth and the milk, then simmer gently while stirring for 8 minutes. • Season the sauce with the lemon juice, the vinegar, the bay leaf and the salt and pepper. • Cover and cook the liver slices in the sauce over a low heat for 3 to 4 minutes. The liver is done when it has turned gray. • Stir in the crème fraîche and remove the bay leaf. • Serve with mashed potatoes and a green salad.

## Steak and Kidney Pie

**Slightly difficult, an English specialty**

Soaking time: 1 hour
Preparation time: 45 minutes
Baking time: 1 hour
Serves: 6 people

| |
|---|
| 5 oz. frozen puff pastry |
| 1 lb. calf kidneys |
| 1 lb. sirloin |
| 1 medium onion |
| ½ bunch parsley |
| 3 tbs. flour |
| ½ tsp. salt |
| ¼ tsp. freshly ground black pepper |
| 2 tbs. beef or bacon fat |
| 6 tbs. dry sherry |
| ½ tsp. Worcestershire sauce |
| 1 egg yolk |
| 1 tbs. milk |

Thaw the puff pastry at room temperature. • Remove any fat and vessels from the kidneys, cut into pieces and place in cold water for 1 hour. Change the water frequently. • Rinse the kidneys, dry and cut into small cubes. • Rinse the sirloin, dry and cut similarly into small cubes. • Peel and finely chop the onion. Wash the parsley and spin dry. Remove any tough stems and finely chop the leaves. • Mix the flour with the salt and pepper and dredge the meat cubes in it. • Heat the beef fat in a large pan and sauté the onion until translucent. Add the meat and kidney cubes, brown until uniformly golden and remove from the heat. • Warm 1 cup of water and mix with the sherry, the Worcestershire sauce and the parsley. • Blend the seasoning

liquid with the meat and fill a pie pan or flat ovenproof dish with the mixture. • Preheat the oven to 425°. • Unroll the puff pastry on a lightly floured surface slightly larger than the baking dish and then place over the meat filling. The dough should extend about 1 inch past the edge of the dish. • Press the edge of the dough tightly to the dish. Cut a small round hole in the middle of the crust, so that steam can escape. • Make decorative shapes out of any leftover dough. • Blend the egg yolk with the milk and glaze the crust with it. Place the decorations on the crust and glaze. • Bake the pie on the middle rack of the oven for 30 minutes. Then reduce the temperature to 350° and cook an

additional 30 minutes. • Serve the pie while still hot in the dish. • Serve with chicory salad or oak leaf salad.

## Viennese Calf Lung Goulash

### An Austrian specialty

Preparation time: 20 minutes
Cooking time: 1 hour
Weighting time: 12 hours
Finishing time: 25 minutes

| |
|---|
| 1½ lbs. calf lung |
| 2 onions |
| 2 carrots |
| 1 parsley root |
| ½ cup celery root |
| 6 white peppercorns |
| 2 cloves garlic |
| 1 bay leaf |
| ½ tsp. salt |
| ½ tsp. dried thyme |
| 3 tbs. flour |
| Grated rind of ½ lemon |
| 2 tbs. capers |
| 1 tbs. lemon juice |
| Salt and freshly ground white pepper to taste |
| Sugar to taste |
| 2 tbs. butter |
| 4 tbs. cream |

Rinse the lung. • Peel, wash and cut the vegetables into pieces. • Boil 1½ quarts of water with the spices and the vegetables. • Place the lung in the boiling water. Frequently skim any foam that collects. Cover and simmer gently for 1 hour. • Drain the lung. Strain the cooking liquid and place 2 cups in the refrigerator. Reduce the remainder and freeze. • Press the lung between two weighted chopping boards for 12 hours. • Cut the lung into strips ¼-inch wide. • Blend the flour with cold water and mix into the 2 cups of cooking broth. Simmer gently 10 minutes while stirring. • Season the sauce with the lemon rind, the capers, the lemon juice, salt, pepper and sugar. It should have a strong sweet-and-sour flavor. • Warm the lung in the sauce over a low heat. • Beat the butter in small pieces and the cream into the sauce with a whisk. • Serve with dumplings.

## Venetian-Style Calf Liver

**An Italian specialty, famous recipe**

Preparation time: 40 minutes

| | |
|---|---|
| 1¼ lbs. calf liver | |
| 4 small shallots | |
| ½ bunch parsley | |
| 2 tbs. coconut oil | |
| ½ cup dry white wine | |
| ½ tsp. salt | |
| ¼ tsp. freshly ground white pepper | |
| 3 tbs. ice cold butter | |

**R**inse the calf liver in cold water, dry and slice thinly. Remove any skin and hard vessels. • Peel the shallots and slice in thin rings. Wash the parsley and spin dry; remove any tough stems and finely chop the leaves. • Heat the coconut oil and sauté the shallots until translucent. Mix the parsley with the shallots and gradually add the white wine. Bring the wine to a boil and add the liver slices. Cover and stew for 4 minutes over low heat. • Season the sauce with salt and pepper. Blend the butter into the sauce with a whisk.

## Veal Kidneys in Cognac Cream

**Easy to prepare**

Cooking time: 40 minutes
Preparation time: 30 minutes

| | |
|---|---|
| 1¼ lbs. calf kidneys | |
| 1 tbs. flour | |
| ½ tsp. salt | |
| 1 medium onion | |
| 2 tbs. coconut oil | |
| ½ cup hot beef broth | |
| ½ cup crème fraîche | |
| 1 egg yolk | |
| 2 tbs. freshly grated Swiss cheese | |
| ⅛ tsp. freshly ground white pepper | |
| 2 tbs. cognac | |
| 1 tsp. freshly chopped parsley | |

**H**alve the calf kidneys horizontally and remove any skin or hard vessels. • Cover the kidneys with cold water and soak 40 minutes; change the water 3 times while soaking. • Dry the kidneys and cut into slices about ½-inch thick. Mix the salt with the flour and dredge the kidney slices in it. • Peel and dice the onion. • Heat the coconut oil in a pan, sauté the onion until golden and add the kidneys. Brown over medium heat 4 minutes, turning frequently. • Add the beef broth and bring to a boil. Remove from the heat. • Blend the crème fraîche with the egg yolk and the cheese and mix into the sauce. Season with salt, pepper and the cognac, then sprinkle with parsley. • Serve with mashed potatoes.

## Beef Tongue in Burgundy Sauce

**Famous recipe, requires some time**

Preparation time: 40 minutes
Cooking time: 3½ hours
Serves: 8 people

| |
|---|
| 1 beef tongue (4½ lbs.) |
| 2 bunches soup herbs |
| 1 large onion |
| 1 small leek |
| 1 tsp. salt |
| 2 tbs. butter |
| 2 tsp. sugar |
| 3 tbs. flour |
| 1 bay leaf |
| 5 juniper berries |
| 1 cup red Burgundy wine |
| 4 tsp. currant jelly |
| 8 tbs. crème fraîche |
| ¼ tsp. freshly ground black pepper |
| Pinch of hot paprika |

**R**inse the tongue under cold water, being careful to brush the top of the tongue thoroughly. • Wash, trim and chop the herbs. Peel and quarter the onion. Trim the dark green ends and the root end from the leek. Halve the leek, wash and cut in pieces. • Bring 2 quarts of water to a rolling boil with the prepared vegetables and salt. Place the tongue in the boiling water and boil 20 minutes in the open pot. Skim repeatedly any foam that collects during this time. • Cover the pot, leaving a small opening, and reduce the temperature. Cook the tongue for 3 hours in the water barely at a boil. The tongue is done when the tip can be pierced easily with a fork. • Lift the tongue from the liquid, douse with cold water and remove the skin, the tongue bone and the gullet. • Strain the cooking liquid and reserve 2 cups. • Place the tongue back in the pot and keep warm in the remaining liquid. • Melt the butter for the sauce in a small pot. Sprinkle with the sugar and caramelize until golden while stirring. Sprinkle the flour in and stir until brown, but do not let the roux get too dark or the sauce will taste bitter. • Gradually stir the reserved broth into the roux, add the bay leaf and juniper berries, cover and simmer over low heat for 20 minutes. • Stir the Burgundy wine into the sauce. Heat but do not allow to boil. Mix the currant jelly with the crème fraîche and blend into the sauce. Season with salt, pepper and paprika. • Dab the tongue dry and cut into diagonal slices. Arrange on a serving platter with some of the sauce. Serve the remaining sauce separately. • Serve with buttered noodles and creamed spinach or potato croquettes and Brussels sprouts with bread crumbs.

## Pot Roast

**Famous recipe, requires some time**

Preparation time: 30 minutes
Cooking time: 1½ hours

| |
|---|
| 1¾ lbs. beef round roast |
| 2 carrots |
| 2 onions |
| 2 oz. unsalted bacon |
| 4 white peppercorns |
| 1 sprig parsley |
| Salt |
| 1 tbs. butter |
| 1 tbs. flour |
| 2 tbs. tomato paste |
| Freshly ground white pepper |
| ½ tsp. mustard |
| ½ tsp. sugar |
| 6 tbs. sour cream |

Remove any skin from the meat, rinse and dry. • Peel and dice the vegetables. Cube the bacon. • Boil 1½ cups water. • Fry the bacon and sear the roast on all sides in the hot fat. Add the vegetables, peppercorns, parsley and salt, and brown everything for 10 minutes. • Add half of the boiling water and cook the meat covered for 1 hour. Add more hot water as necessary and baste the meat. • Remove and keep the roast warm in the oven. • Add some hot water to the pan and scrape up any drippings. Pour this liquid and the vegetables through a sieve. • Melt the butter and brown the flour in it until golden. Add the tomato paste and the cooking liquid. Add enough water to make 1½ cups liquid. Finish the sauce with the spices and the sour cream. • Carve the roast and pour the sauce over it. Serve with mashed potatoes and red cabbage.

## Beef with Fried Onions

**Famous recipe**

Preparation time: 50 minutes

| |
|---|
| 1 lb. onions |
| 1 tsp. sugar |
| 1½ tsp. salt |
| 2 tbs. butter |
| 4 slices top round beef (5 oz. each) |
| ¼ tsp. freshly ground white pepper |
| 2 tsp. flour |
| 2 tbs. oil |
| 1 cup beef broth |
| 6 tbs. dry red wine |

Slice the onions in rings and mix with the sugar and ½ teaspoon salt. • Melt the butter in a large pan. Sauté the onion rings over low heat for 40 minutes until golden brown. Place to the side. • Rinse and dry the beef, flatten, rub with salt and pepper, then dredge in the flour. • Preheat the oven to 400°. • Heat the oil in a second pan and sear the meat on both sides 1 minute. Reduce the heat and brown the meat on both sides for an additional 3 minutes. Keep warm in the oven. • Add the beef broth to the pan and scrape the drippings loose. Add the red wine and season the sauce. • Reheat the onion rings, arrange on the beef and pour the sauce around the meat. • Serve with potatoes and salad.

# Festive
# Roasts

## Veal Kidney Roast

**Famous recipe, requires some time**

Preparation time: 30 minutes
Cooking time: 1½ hours
Finishing time: 15 minutes
Serves: 6 people

| |
| --- |
| 2 lbs. veal kidney roast |
| 1 garlic clove |
| 1 medium onion |
| 1 large carrot |
| 2 leeks |
| Salt |
| Freshly ground white pepper |
| 5 tbs. oil |
| 2 cups beef broth |
| 1 bunch basil |
| 1 cup crème fraîche |

Have the butcher roll and tie the proper pieces of meat for the kidney roast. • Preheat the oven to 425°. • Peel and halve the garlic clove, then throughly rub a roasting pan with it. • Peel the onion and cut into eighths. Peel and wash the carrot, then cut into slivers (not too thin). Wash and trim the leeks and cut into medium slices. • Rinse the kidney roast under cold water, dry and rub on all sides with salt and pepper. • Heat the oil in the roasting pan on top of the stove and sear the meat on all sides over a high heat (roughly 10 minutes). • Place the prepared onion, leeks and carrot around the roast. Cook the roast in the oven on the middle rack for 1½ hours. •

Heat the meat broth and, as soon as the vegetables in the roaster begin to brown, pour some of the broth over them. Scrape up any drippings and baste often for a juicier roast. • During the entire cooking time continue pouring hot beef broth over the vegetables. If no broth remains, then use a little hot water. • Place the cooked roast on a warmed platter and cover loosely with aluminum foil. Keep in the oven (the heat should be off) so that the internal juices penetrate the roast evenly and do not escape during carving. • In the meantime add a little hot water to the roasting pan and scrape up the drippings, then strain into a smaller pan and keep warm. • Wash the basil,

spin dry, remove any tough stems and finely chop. • Season the sauce with salt and pepper, blend in the crème fraîche and sprinkle with basil. • Carve the roast and pour a little sauce over it. Serve the remaining sauce separately. • Small bread dumplings and Brussels sprouts or broad, buttered noodles and a chicory salad with oranges and kiwis are good with veal kidney roast.

## Veal Shoulder with Wheat Germ Bread

**Nutritious**

Preparation time: 30 minutes
Cooking time: 1½ hours

| |
| --- |
| 2 lbs. veal shoulder |
| ½ tsp. freshly ground white pepper |
| 1 bunch soup herbs |
| 3 slices wheat germ bread |
| 1 bay leaf |
| 1 tsp. chopped basil |
| ½ cup vegetable broth |
| ⅔ cup cream |
| ½ tsp. sea salt |
| 1 tsp. sweet paprika |
| 1 tbs. fresh dill, chopped |
| Juice of ½ lemon |

**R**inse the meat, dry and remove any skin. Rub with the pepper. • Preheat the oven to 425°. • Wash the soup herbs, trim and chop. Cube the bread. • Place the meat in the roasting bag and add the prepared ingredients with the bay leaf and basil; then add the vegetable broth. Tightly close the bag and pierce the top side several times. • Place the meat in the cold roaster and cook on the second rack in the oven for 1½ hours. Reduce the temperature to 350° after 45 minutes. • Keep the roast warm on a platter in the turned-off oven. • Pour the cooking juices through a sieve, blend with the cream, salt, paprika, dill and lemon juice, then heat. Serve with the roast.

## Veal Roast with Bell Peppers

**Slightly expensive**

Preparation time: 40 minutes
Cooking time: 1 hour and 20 minutes

| |
| --- |
| 1¾ lbs. veal center-cut roast |
| Salt |
| Freshly ground white pepper |
| ½ tsp. dried oregano |
| 3 onions |
| 1 lb. red bell peppers |
| ½ cup dry white wine |
| ½ cup cream |
| 1 tbs. Worcestershire sauce |
| 1 tsp. sweet paprika |

**P**reheat the oven to 425°. • Rinse and dry the meat, then rub with the spices. • Peel and coarsely chop the onions. Wash, dry and trim the bell peppers, then cut into strips. • Place the meat with the vegetables in a roasting bag, add the wine, close tightly and pierce the top of the bag several times. • Place the roast in the cold roaster and cook on the middle rack of the oven for 1 hour and 20 minutes. • Keep the roast warm on a platter in the turned-off oven. • Puree the vegetables with the cooking juices and the cream. Reduce until the sauce is smooth, then season with salt, pepper, Worcestershire sauce and paprika. • Carve the roast and serve the sauce separately.

## Breast of Veal with Mushroom Stuffing

### Requires some time

Preparation time: 40 minutes
Cooking time: 2 hours
Serves: 6 people

2 lbs. boned breast of veal
Salt
Freshly ground black pepper
3 stale rolls
1 onion
1 cup mushrooms
¼ cup butter
1 bunch parsley
1 garlic clove
4 slices bacon
¼ cup Emmenthaler cheese
2 eggs
1 tbs. each flour and bread crumbs
½ cup dry white wine
2 carrots
12 shallots
4 tbs. crème fraîche

Cut a pocket in the breast of veal and rub with salt and pepper. • Soften the rolls in water. • Chop the onion and slice the mushrooms. • Sauté the onion in 1 tablespoon of butter until translucent. Add the mushrooms and chopped parsley and sauté for 3 minutes. • Chop the garlic and the bacon; grate the cheese. Mix with the eggs, the flour, the bread crumbs, the rolls (after pressing the water out) and the mushroom mixture. Season with salt and pepper. • Fill the pocket with the farce and sew the opening shut. • Place the breast of veal in a Dutch oven and drizzle with the remaining butter, melted. • Add the wine (reserve a little) and ½ cup water to the pan and place on the middle rack of the oven. • Heat the oven to 400°. • Cut up the peeled vegetables and place around the roast after 1¼ hours. • Add some wine and cook the veal another 45 minutes. • Strain the cooking juices and blend with the crème fraîche. Serve with the veal.

## Breast of Veal with Stuffing

### Nutritious

Preparation time: 30 minutes
Cooking time: 2 hours

2 lbs. lean breast of veal
½ tsp. freshly ground white pepper
1 large onion
1 large carrot
5 tbs. butter
¼ cup wheat flour
1 tsp. each granulated bouillon and paprika
2 tbs. chopped parsley
1 egg
1 tsp. sea salt
1 cup dry white wine
6 tbs. cream
1 tbs. lemon juice
1 tbs. chopped lemon herb

Cut a pocket in the meat and rub with pepper. • Chop the vegetables and sauté in 2 tablespoons of butter. • Mix the wheat flour with ½ cup water and the bouillon, bring to a boil and soak for 10 minutes. • Mix half of the meat with some parsley, the egg and salt. Fill the meat pocket and sew shut. • Brown the meat in the remaining butter, salt and add the wine. Roast in the oven at 425° for 1¼ hours. • Mix the remaining meat with some water with the pan juices and roast an additional 35 minutes. • Blend the strained liquid with the cream, lemon juice and lemon herbs. Serve the sauce separately.

## Shank of Veal in Cream and Wine Sauce

**Nutritious, requires some time**

Preparation time: 40 minutes
Cooking time: 2 hours

| |
|---|
| 3½ lbs. veal shank |
| ¼ tsp. freshly ground white pepper |
| ½ cup each carrots, celery root and leek |
| 2 garlic cloves |
| 4 tbs. oil |
| 1 cup dry white wine |
| Juice of ½ lemon |
| 1 tsp. sea salt |
| ⅛ tsp. cayenne pepper |
| 1 cup cream |
| 5 tbs. tomato paste |
| 2 tbs. whole-wheat flour |
| 2 tbs. chopped basil |
| 2 tbs. chopped parsley |

Skin the veal shank, rinse under cold water, dry and rub with pepper. • Trim, wash and chop the vegetables. Chop the garlic. • Preheat the oven to 425°. • Sear the shank evenly in the oil in a roaster until crispy brown. Add and sauté the vegetables briefly. • Add ½ cup wine and the lemon juice to the meat, sprinkle with salt and cayenne pepper. Cover and cook on the second rack of the oven for 1¾ hours. Little by little add the remaining wine. • Blend the tomato paste, flour, basil and a little water into the cream until smooth. Fifteen minutes before the shank finishes cooking, stir the cream mixture into the pan juices and continue cooking the meat uncovered. • Keep the shank warm. • Season the sauce and add the parsley. Serve separately with the veal shank.

## Beef Wellington

### Slightly difficult, slightly expensive

Preparation time: 1¼ hours
Cooking time: 50 minutes
Serves: 6 people

| |
| --- |
| 14 oz. frozen puff pastry |
| 5 tbs. butter |
| 2 onions |
| 1¾ cups mushrooms |
| 3 tbs. dry sherry |
| 1 tsp. each salt and freshly ground white pepper |
| 1 pinch each cayenne pepper and freshly ground nutmeg |
| 2 lbs. beef tenderloin |
| 3 tbs. clarified butter |
| Flour for the work surface |
| 1 egg white |
| 2 egg yolks |

**R**emove the puff pastry from the package and thaw. • Place 3 tablespoons butter in the freezer compartment. • Peel and finely chop the onions. Clean and finely chop the mushrooms. • Melt the remaining butter in a pan and sauté the onions until translucent. Add the mushrooms and sauté until nearly all the liquid has evaporated. • Mix the onion-mushroom mixture with the sherry and cool. • Cut the frozen butter into bits. Puree the mushroom mixture, adding the butter bits while blending. • Season the puree well with salt, pepper, cayenne and nutmeg. Cool. • Rinse the beef, dry and remove any skin or fat. • Heat the clarified butter in a roaster and brown the meat well on all sides for 15 minutes, cool and rub with salt and pepper. •

Preheat the oven to 425°. • Roll out the puff pastry on a floured surface to a square the thickness of a knife blade. Cut strips from the edges for the garnish. Brush the edge (½ inch) of the pastry with egg white. • Spread half of the mushroom farce on the pastry, lay the meat in the middle and cover with the remaining farce. Wrap the pastry around the meat and press the seams together. • Rinse a baking sheet with cold water, but do not dry. Place the meat with the long seam down on the baking sheet. Cut the remaining strips with a pastry wheel. • Beat the egg yolks and brush over the pastry, then position the pastry strips and brush them. • Bake on the middle rack of the oven until the pastry crust is golden brown. This takes approximately 40 min-

utes. • Turn off the oven and let the meat rest in the oven with the door open for 10 minutes. • Cut the Beef Wellington into finger-thick slices and arrange on a warmed platter. • Serve with a large mixed salad.

## Roast Beef with Yorkshire Pudding

**English specialty, slightly expensive**

Preparation time: 40 minutes
Resting time: 1 hour
Cooking time: 40 minutes
Serves: 6 people

For the Yorkshire pudding:

2 cups milk

4 eggs

1⅛ cups flour

⅛ tsp. each salt and freshly ground white pepper

1 pinch freshly ground nutmeg

1 tbs. suet or bacon fat

For the roast beef:

2 lbs. roast beef

½ tsp. freshly ground black pepper

1 tbs. Worcestershire sauce

2 tbs. dry sherry

½ tsp. green peppercorns

4 tbs. oil

1 tsp. salt

Scald and then cool the milk. • Beat the eggs in a bowl, sift the flour in and beat well into the eggs. Gradually beat in the milk. Season the dough with the salt, pepper and nutmeg and let stand in the refrigerator 1 hour. • Rinse and dry the roast beef. With a sharp knife, cut a diamond pattern into the layer of fat, taking care not to cut into the meat beneath. The cuts allow fat to drip onto the pudding while baking. • Mix the pepper with the Worcestershire sauce, sherry, the crushed green peppercorns and the oil. • Rub the meat with this mixture, then place in a bowl, cover and marinate for 30 minutes. Turn the meat frequently while marinating. • Preheat the oven to 475°. • Oil a grilling rack and rinse a pan for the pudding with cold water. • Dab the roast beef dry and rub with the salt. Place the meat on the middle rack of the oven and the pudding pan on the lowest rack. Cook the meat 15 minutes. • Beat the pudding dough well once again. Heat the beef fat and mix into the meat juices which have collected in the pudding pan. • Pour the dough into the pudding pan and smooth the surface. Place on the lower rack and bake the Yorkshire pudding under the roast beef. • After 10 minutes reduce the heat to 400° and cook another 15 minutes. • Let the roast beef rest on a warm platter in the turned-off oven for 10 minutes so that the juices penetrate the meat. • Cut the Yorkshire pudding into strips. Carve the roast beef. • Good with broccoli with almond butter and grilled tomatoes garnished with basil leaves.

Tip: If the roast beef gives easily to finger pressure, then it is still red. If it does not give so easily, then it is pink inside. A meat thermometer is useful: if it reads 115° then the meat is still red. At 140° it is pink.

## Beef Brisket with Horseradish

**Requires some time**

Preparation time: 30 minutes
Cooking time: 2½ hours
Serves: 6 people

3½ lbs. beef brisket

½ tsp. each salt and freshly ground pepper

3 slices smoked bacon

4 shallots

2 carrots

½ celery root

1 bay leaf

½ cup fresh horseradish

1 pinch each salt and sugar

1 tbs. vinegar

1 cup cream

**P**reheat the oven to 350°. •
Rinse the meat, dry, rub with the salt and pepper and cover with the bacon slices. • Peel, wash and coarsely chop the vegetables. • Place the meat, the vegetables and the bay leaf in a large roasting bag, close tightly and pierce the surface several times. • Set the meat in a cold roasting pan on the second lowest rack in the oven and roast for 2½ hours. • Peel, wash and finely grate the horseradish. Season with the salt, sugar and vinegar. • Beat the cream until stiff and mix with the horseradish. • Put the meat with any juices on a platter, carve and serve with the horseradish cream.

## Beef Tenderloin in Savoy Cabbage

**Slightly expensive**

Preparation time: 40 minutes
Cooking time: 40 minutes
Serves: 6 people

2 lbs. beef tenderloin

2 tbs. clarified butter

¼ tsp. each salt and freshly ground white pepper

3 veal sausages

2 tbs. chopped parsley

1 tsp. dried thyme

10 large savoy cabbage leaves

½ cup beef broth

¾ cup heavy cream

1 tsp. cornstarch

**S**ear the tenderloin in the hot clarified butter. Salt, pepper and set aside, covered. • Preheat the oven to 425°. • Mix the veal sausage meat with the herbs. • Blanch the cabbage leaves for 5 minutes. Cut the middle ribs and flatten into squares. Spread with the sausage mixture. • Wrap the tenderloin in the leaves and tie together with kitchen string. • Place the meat in a roasting bag, add the broth and close tightly. Pierce the surface of the bag several times. • Place the meat in a cold roaster on the second rack of the oven and roast for 30 minutes. After 15 minutes reduce the heat to 350°. • Pour the cooking juices into a pot and bind with the cream blended with the cornstarch. Serve the sauce separately.

## Chateaubriand in Puff Pastry

**Famous recipe, slightly difficult**

Preparation time: 40 minutes
Cooking time: 25 minutes

| | |
|---|---|
| 10 oz. frozen puff pastry | |
| ⅔ cup mushrooms | |
| 1¼ lbs. beef tenderloin | |
| ½ tsp. salt | |
| ⅛ tsp. freshly ground white pepper | |
| 2 tbs. butter | |
| ½ cup cooked ham | |
| 1 egg | |
| 1 tbs. cream | |
| 1 egg yolk | |
| 7 tbs. butter | |

Thaw the puff pastry. • Clean and thinly slice the mushrooms. • Rinse and dry the tenderloin. Remove any skin and fat. Pound flat (to about 1 inch thick). Rub with salt and pepper and sear in the butter on both sides for 2 minutes over a high heat. Cool. • Sauté the mushrooms in the remaining butter for 2 minutes. Salt and pepper, then remove from the pan. • Preheat the oven to 425°. • Roll out the puff pastry into 2 oval crusts. Place 1 crust on a baking sheet rinsed in cold water. Cover with the ham and half the mushrooms, lay the meat on top and cover with the remaining mushrooms. • Blend the egg with the cream and use it to paint the edge of the dough. Lay the second crust over the tenderloin and press the edges together. • Cut a circle of dough 1 inch in diameter from the crust so that steam can escape. Brush the crust with the egg mixture. • Bake on the second rack of the oven for 12 minutes. Let rest in the turned-off oven with the door open for 10 minutes. • Blend the egg yolk with the butter, warm and serve as a sauce with the tenderloin.

## Sauerbraten

**Famous recipe**

Preparation time: 30 minutes
Marinating time: 2 days
Cooking time: 40 minutes

| |
| --- |
| 2 lbs. beef (heel of round) |
| 1 carrot |
| 1 parsley root |
| ¾ cup celery root |
| 4 each whole allspice and black peppercorns |
| 1 bay leaf |
| 2 sprigs fresh thyme |
| 1 cup Burgundy wine |
| ½ cup red wine vinegar |
| 1 tsp. salt |
| ⅛ tsp. freshly ground black pepper |
| 3 slices bacon |
| 4 tbs. coconut oil |
| 2 tbs. tomato paste |

**R**emove any skin and fat from the meat. • Peel, wash and finely chop the vegetables. Add to the meat with the spices and the wine. • Bring the vinegar to a boil with ½ cup water, cool and pour over the meat. Cover and marinate in the refrigerator for 2 days, turning frequently. • Preheat the oven to 425°. • Dry the meat and rub with salt and pepper. Strain the marinade. • Cube the bacon and fry in a roasting pan. Add the oil and sear the meat well. Add the vegetables and spices from the marinade, sauté lightly, then stir in the tomato paste. Pour in the marinade. • Cover the meat and cook on the lowest rack of the oven for 40 minutes. • Keep the roast warm. • Pour the sauce through a sieve, season and serve with the roast. • Serve with red cabbage and mashed potatoes.

## Sirloin Roast with Vegetables

**Slightly expensive**

Preparation time: 35 minutes
Cooking time: 30 minutes

| |
| --- |
| 1¾ lbs. sirloin roast |
| 1½ tsp. salt |
| ¼ tsp. freshly ground white pepper |
| 1 cucumber |
| 1 cauliflower |
| 4 tomatoes |
| 2 shallots |
| 2 tbs. coconut oil |
| 2 sprigs fresh tarragon |
| 1 tbs. sweet paprika |
| ¾ cup crème fraîche |
| 2 tbs. chopped chives |

**R**ub the meat with 1 teaspoon salt and the pepper. • Chop the cucumber in 1-inch cubes. Separate the cauliflower into florets, trim the stems and wash. • Cut a cross into the round end of the tomatoes. Peel the shallots and cut into eighths. • Preheat the oven to 400°. • Heat the oil in a roaster and sear the meat. After 10 minutes sprinkle the vegetables and the chopped tarragon next to the meat and add the tomatoes. Blend the crème fraîche with the remaining salt and the paprika and pour over the vegetables. • Roast the sirloin on the lowest rack of the oven for 30 minutes. Sprinkle with the chives before serving.

## Wild Rabbit in Sour Cream

**Requires some time**

Marinating time: 24 hours
Preparation time: 20 minutes
Cooking time: 1 hour

| |
|---|
| 1 wild rabbit, about 2 lbs. |
| ¼ tsp. freshly ground black pepper |
| 2 cups sour cream |
| ¼ cup graham cracker crumbs |
| 1 tbs. mildly spicy mustard |
| 1 tsp. each sea salt, fresh chopped thyme and crushed juniper berries |
| 3 tbs. butter |
| 1 cup dry rosé wine |

Cut the meat into 8 pieces, rub with half of the pepper and place in a bowl. Cover with the sour cream and marinate in a covered dish in the refrigerator 24 hours. • Preheat the oven to 425°. • Scrape the sour cream from the meat and blend with the graham cracker crumbs, the mustard, salt, thyme, juniper berries and the remaining pepper. • Place the rabbit in a roaster and cover with the sour cream mixture. Dot with half the butter in bits and add the wine. • Bake the rabbit on the second lowest rack in the oven for 1 hour. Baste every 10 minutes with the sauce. • After 30 minutes turn the meat and dot with the remaining butter. • Keep the rabbit warm on a platter in the turned-off oven. • Deglaze the pan with a little hot water and serve the sauce separately with the rabbit.

## Hare in Juniper Cream

**Slightly expensive, famous recipe**

Preparation time: 20 minutes
Cooking time: 25 minutes
Finishing time: 15 minutes

| |
|---|
| 2 larded wild hare backs (1 lb. each) |
| 1 tsp. salt |
| 2 tsp. sweet paprika |
| 2 onions |
| ¼ cup clarified butter |
| ½ cup sour cream |
| ½ tsp. sugar |
| 2 tbs. tomato paste |
| 4 tbs. currant jelly |
| 10 juniper berries |
| 1 cup dry red wine |

Preheat the oven to 425°. • Rub the hare backs with the salt and paprika. • Peel the onions and cut into eighths. • Heat the clarified butter in a roaster. Sauté the onions in it, then add the meat and roast on the second rack of the oven for 25 minutes. • Wrap the hare backs in doubled aluminum foil and let rest 10 minutes in the turned-off oven, with the door open. • Deglaze the meat juices with a little hot water and put in a pot with the onions. Mix in the sour cream, sugar, tomato paste, currant jelly, juniper berries and red wine. Cover and simmer gently 10 minutes. Strain and pour over the hare. • Serve with potato croquettes and chanterelles.

## Roasted Saddle of Venison

### Norwegian specialty, takes some time

Preparation time: 30 minutes
Cooking time: 1½ hours
Serves: 6 people

| |
| --- |
| 1 saddle of venison, about 3½ lbs. |
| 1 tsp. salt |
| ¼ tsp. freshly ground white pepper |
| ½ tsp. dried thyme |
| 4 slices fat bacon |
| 3 tbs. butter |
| 1 tbs. flour |
| ½ cup hot beef broth |
| 6 tbs. heavy cream |
| 1 tsp. soy sauce |
| 1 tbs. currant jelly |
| ¼ cup goat cheese |

**P**reheat the oven to 325°. • Remove any skin from the venison and rub with 1 teaspoon salt, the pepper and thyme. Cover with the bacon slices. • Wrap the venison in a large, doubled piece of extra-heavy aluminum foil, seal the edges tightly and roast the meat on the second lowest rack of the oven for 1 hour. • Open the foil. • Raise the oven temperature to 425° and cook an additional 30 minutes. • After 15 minutes remove the bacon and discard. • Melt the butter and sprinkle the flour in, then stir until smooth. Add the beef broth and simmer gently 10 minutes. • Add the meat juices from the foil, the cream, soy sauce, jelly and remaining salt. Add the cubed cheese to the no longer boiling sauce and blend until melted. • Carve the saddle of venison and serve with the sauce. • Good with red cabbage and mashed potatoes.

# Rabbit with Peppers

**Spanish specialty, requires some time**

Preparation time: 50 minutes
Cooking time: 45 minutes
Serves: 8 people

| 2 rabbits, about 3 lbs. each |
| 2 tsp. salt |
| 1½ tsp. freshly ground black pepper |
| 8 tbs. olive oil |
| 1 small piece dried chili pepper |
| 1½ lbs. tomatoes |
| 6 red bell peppers |
| 6 large onions |
| 5 garlic cloves |
| ⅔ cup black olives |
| 1 cup dry red wine |
| Oil for the pan |

Cut each rabbit into 8 pieces. Rinse each piece, dry and rub with salt and pepper. • Heat part of the olive oil in a large pan, add the piece of chili pepper and sear the rabbit well in portions on all sides. The pieces should be crispy and brown. • Remove the chili and place the meat to the side. • Preheat the oven to 400°. • Cut a cross into the round ends of the tomatoes, plunge briefly into boiling water and skin, then quarter. Remove the stem portions. • Rinse and dry the bell peppers and remove the seeds and membranes. Cut the peppers into broad strips. • Peel and quarter the onions. Peel and finely chop the garlic. Pit and halve the olives. • Sauté the onion quarters and chopped garlic in the remaining oil until translucent. • Add the bell pepper strips, the olives and the tomato quarters, sauté briefly, then pour in the red wine. Season with salt and pepper. • Oil an ovenproof pan (the drippings pan from the oven) with some olive oil. • Arrange the vegetables in the pan and distribute the meat on top. Bake on the second lowest rack of the oven for about 45 minutes. • During the cooking time add wine if needed, so that the vegetables do not become dry. • Serve this decorative dish in the pan or on a preheated serving platter. • Good with fresh warm French bread and the same wine used for the vegetables.

Tip: The spiciness of the dish is determined by the chili pepper. If spicy food is desired, use a larger piece of the chili and, if desired, remove it only after the dish is cooked. In any case, use the chili pepper carefully so that the aroma of the vegetables is not overwhelmed. If one does not care for spicy foods, omit the chili and season the rabbit with 1 pinch of cayenne pepper.

## Alsatian Lamb Roast

**French specialty**

Marinating time: 4 hours
Preparation time: 30 minutes
Cooking time: 1 hour
Serves: 6 people

| | |
|---|---|
| 1 garlic clove |
| ½ tsp. each whole allspice, white peppercorns and whole coriander |
| ⅛ tsp. each dried marjoram and thyme |
| 3½ lbs. lamb roast |
| 3 tbs. clarified butter |
| 2 sprigs fresh rosemary |
| ½ cup hot beef broth |
| ½ tsp. each salt and freshly ground black pepper |
| 1 cup dry red wine |
| ½ lemon |
| 1 cup cream |

Crush the garlic with the spices and herbs in a mortar. Rub the lamb with the mixture and marinate covered 4 hours. • Preheat the oven to 400°. • Heat the clarified butter in a roaster. Sear the meat well, then add the rosemary, the broth, salt and pepper. Roast the meat covered in the oven for 1 hour. Add wine as needed. • Wash and thinly peel the lemon. Cut the rind in fine strips. Squeeze the juice. • Keep the lamb roast warm. • Strain the cooking juices and blend with the cream. Reduce slightly and mix in the lemon rind and juice. Season with salt and pepper. • Carve the roast and serve with the sauce.

## Lamb Roast with an Herb Crust

**Slightly expensive**

Preparation time: 30 minutes
Cooking time: 45 minutes
Serves: 6 people

| | |
|---|---|
| 3½ lbs. lamb roast |
| 1 tsp. each salt and white pepper |
| ¼ cup butter |
| Juice of 2 lemons |
| 2 bunches of parsley |
| 1 bunch of peppermint |
| 3 garlic cloves |
| 3 slices white bread, crusts removed |
| 3 tbs. oil |
| 2 tbs. mustard |
| ⅔ cup crème fraîche |
| 3 tbs. kneaded butter |

Preheat the oven to 425°. • Rub the meat with salt and pepper, place in flat roasting pan and dribble with 2 tablespoons melted butter. Roast 45 minutes on the second rack of the oven. • Mix the lemon juice with ½ cup water and pour gradually over the roast. • Finely chop the herbs and garlic and mix with the bread crumbs, oil, mustard and remaining butter. Spread this over the roast halfway through the cooking time. • Keep the done roast warm. Strain the cooking juices and add water to make 2 cups of liquid. Season with salt and pepper, mix with the crème fraîche and bind with the kneaded butter. • Carve the lamb roast and serve with the sauce.

## Leg of Lamb au Gratin

### Requires some time

Preparation time: 40 minutes
Marinating time: 12 hours
Cooking time: 1½ hours
Serves: 6 people

| |
|---|
| 1 3½ lb. leg of lamb |
| 5 garlic cloves |
| 1 sprig fresh thyme |
| ¼ tsp. freshly ground black pepper |
| Juice of 1 lemon |
| 4 tbs. oil |
| 1¾ lbs. zucchini |
| 2 onions |
| 1¾ lbs. potatoes |
| 1 tsp. salt |
| ¼ cup freshly grated Emmenthaler cheese |
| ½ cup crème fraîche |
| 1 bunch basil |

**P**ierce the lamb at regular intervals and insert slivers of garlic from 4 cloves. Cover the lamb with a mixture of the chopped thyme, pepper, lemon juice and 2 tablespoons of oil and marinate covered for 12 hours. • Preheat the oven to 350°. • Wash the zucchini. Peel the onions and potatoes and cut all the vegetables into slices. • Rub the leg of lamb with salt and brown in the remaining oil on the range top for 10 minutes. • Place the meat in an ovenproof dish and surround with the vegetables. Roast on the lowest rack of the oven 1½ hours. • After 1 hour sprinkle the cheese over the vegetables. • Puree the crème fraîche with the remaining crushed garlic clove, the basil, some salt and pepper and serve with the lamb.

## Crown Roast of Lamb

### Slightly difficult

Marinating time: 16 hours
Preparation time: 30 minutes
Cooking time: 40 minutes
Serves: 6 people

| |
|---|
| 4½ lbs. crown roast of lamb |
| 4 garlic cloves |
| 2 shallots |
| 2 sprigs fresh thyme |
| ½ tsp. each dried sage and black pepper |
| 2 tbs. sesame oil |
| ½ tsp. salt |
| 2 tbs. coconut oil |
| 1 onion |
| 1 carrot |
| 1 parsley root |
| ½ cup celery root |
| ½ cup leek |
| ½ cup each dry red wine and beef broth |
| ⅔ cup heavy cream |

**T**ie the crown roast. • Chop 2 garlic cloves, the shallots and the thyme. Mix with the sage, pepper and oil. Brush the roast with the mixture, then wrap in aluminum foil and marinate 16 hours. • Preheat the oven to 425°. • Scrape the seasoning mixture from the meat and reserve. • Salt the meat and roast in the hot coconut oil for 40 minutes in the oven. • Trim and chop the vegetables. After 20 minutes baking time, sprinkle them around the roast. Baste frequently with the wine and broth. • Let the done roast stand 15 minutes. • Deglaze the cooking juices with the remaining broth and strain with the vegetables. Season with the cream, the remaining crushed garlic clove and the seasoning mixture from the marinade.

## Stuffed Breast of Lamb

**Nutritious, slightly difficult**

Preparation time: 30 minutes
Cooking time: 1¼ hours

| | |
|---|---|
| 2 onions | |
| 2 garlic cloves | |
| 1 carrot | |
| 4 tbs. olive oil | |
| 1 tbs. each coarse ground oats, rye, barley and green rye | |
| ½ tsp. each sea salt and freshly ground black pepper | |
| 1 pinch cayenne pepper | |
| 1 egg | |
| 2 tbs. fresh mixed herbs, chopped | |
| 2 lbs. breast of lamb, prepared for stuffing | |
| 1 cup dry red wine | |
| 2 tsp. granulated bouillon | |
| 6 tbs. cream | |

**P**eel and finely chop the onions and the garlic cloves. • Clean the carrot and finely chop. • Heat 2 tablespoons of oil and sauté the vegetables until the onions are translucent. • Add the grains to the vegetables and sauté briefly. Add ½ cup water, the salt and ⅛ teaspoon pepper and cook 5 minutes over low heat. Cover, remove from heat, let stand 10 minutes. • Preheat the oven to 425°. • Mix the cayenne pepper, the egg and the herbs into the stuffing. • Rub the meat with the remaining pepper and spread the herb stuffing on top. Roll up the breast of lamb and tie with kitchen string. • Heat the remaining oil in a roaster and sear the meat. Add the wine and the bouillon. Roast for 1½ hours in the oven. • Blend the juices with the cream and serve with the roast.

## Rolled Pork Roast with Stuffing

**Requires some time**

Preparation time: 1 hour
Cooking time: 1¼ hours

| |
|---|
| Serves: 8 people |
| 1 onion |
| 3 tbs. bacon fat |
| 1¼ cups savoy cabbage |
| ½ tsp. each salt, freshly ground black pepper and ground caraway |
| 1 tbs. mustard |
| 8 oz. coarse liverwurst |
| 2½ lbs. pork picnic shoulder, cut so that the meat is attached on the broad side |
| 2 bunches soup herbs |
| ½ cup beef broth |

Finely chop the onion and brown in half the bacon fat until translucent. • Cut the savoy cabbage into strips and steam with the onion for 15 minutes. Season with salt, pepper and caraway. Mix with the mustard and liverwurst. • Preheat the oven to 475°. • Rub the meat with the remaining salt, pepper and caraway. Spread the vegetable mixture on the meat, leaving a 1-inch border. Roll up the meat, starting at the broad side, and tie. • Heat the remaining bacon fat in a roaster and sear the meat well on all sides. Set aside. • Trim, wash and chop the soup herbs and add with the meat broth to the rolled roast. Cook for 20 minutes on the second rack of the oven. • Cover the roast, reduce the temperature to 350° and roast an additional hour. • Puree the vegetables with the meat juices and serve with the roast.

## Marinated Cutlet Roast

**Requires some time**

Preparation time: 30 minutes
Marinating time: 24 hours
Cooking time: 1 hour

| |
|---|
| 1¾ lbs. pork cutlet roast |
| 1 tsp. each salt and freshly ground white pepper |
| ½ tsp. each freshly ground nutmeg and sweet paprika |
| ½ cup milk |
| 1 bunch parsley |
| 1 bunch chives |
| 1 sprig fresh rosemary |
| 4 shallots |
| 3 garlic cloves |
| 2 tbs. butter |
| 1 tbs. oil |
| ¾ cup crème fraîche |
| 1 tsp. lemon juice |
| ⅛ tsp. cayenne pepper |

Rub the meat with salt, pepper, nutmeg and paprika and pour the milk over it. • Finely chop the herbs, the shallots and garlic cloves and sprinkle into the milk. • Cover the meat and marinate 24 hours in the refrigerator. • Preheat the oven to 350°. • Dab the meat dry. • Heat the butter and oil in a roaster, sear the meat, then add the marinade. Cook on the second rack of the oven 1 hour. • Let the meat stand in the turned-off oven. • Puree the cooking liquid with the crème fraîche. Season with salt, pepper, lemon juice and cayenne pepper. Carve the meat and pour the sauce over it.

## Pork Roast with Diamond Rind

**Requires some time, inexpensive**

Preparation time: 30 minutes
Cooking time: just under 2 hours
Serves: 6 people

| 1 garlic clove |
| 1 tsp. each salt and freshly ground black pepper |
| ½ tsp. ground caraway |
| 3½ lbs. pork shoulder butt with rind |
| 1 tsp. oil |
| 1 large onion |
| 8 potatoes |
| 1 cup beer |

Chop the garlic clove and crush with the salt, then mix with the pepper and the caraway. Rub the roast with the mixture. • Preheat the oven to 400°. Rub the roast with the oil. • Cut the onion into eighths and place with 2 cups hot water in a flat roasting pan on the lowest oven rack. • Place the meat with the rind down on a grilling rack over the pan and roast 1 hour. • Peel and wash the potatoes, then cut into thin slices. • Remove the meat from the oven. Cut a diamond pattern into the rind. • Reduce the oven temperature to 350°. • Put the potatoes in the pan around the rack and lay the roast with the rind up on the rack. Cook an additional hour. • During the last 20 minutes, baste the roast frequently with the beer. • Let the roast stand 15 minutes, carve and serve with the potatoes, the juices and steamed sauerkraut.

## Pork Roast with Apricots

**Requires some time, inexpensive**

Preparation time: 30 minutes
Cooking time: 2 hours
Serves: 8 people

| 4½ lbs. pork shoulder butt with rind, boned |
| ¾ cup dried apricots |
| 1 tsp. salt |
| ½ tsp. freshly ground black pepper |
| 1 cup cream |
| 1 pinch sugar |
| 2 tsp. cornstarch |
| 2 tbs. slivered almonds |

Preheat the oven to 400°. • Rinse the meat and make a deep slit in the middle of one end. Using the handle of a cooking spoon, widen the hole and extend it the length of the meat. • Stuff the rinsed apricots into the hole. • Cut a crosshatch pattern into the rind and rub with salt and pepper. • Roast the meat in a pan in the oven 2 hours. Every 20 minutes pour some hot water around the roast and baste the meat. • Keep the done roast warm. • Deglaze the pan with a little hot water. Stir in the cream and sugar and bind with the dissolved cornstarch. Mix the slivered almonds into the sauce. • Serve the roast with the sauce, Brussels sprouts and potatoes.

## Grilled Ham Hocks

### Requires some time

Preparation time: 15 minutes
Cooking time: 2½ hours

| |
|---|
| 2 ham hocks, about 2 lbs. each |
| 2 tsp. salt |
| 1 tsp. black peppercorns |
| 1 onion |
| 1 bay leaf |
| 2 cloves |

**R**inse and dry the hocks. •
Bring 2 quarts of water with
the salt and peppercorns to a
rolling boil in a large pot. • Peel
the onion and stud with the bay
leaf and cloves. • Put the hocks
with the onion in the boiling
water and cook over medium
heat 1 hour. Skim any foam as it
collects. • Remove the hocks
from the liquid and cut the skin
at regular intervals with a sharp

knife. Insert a grill skewer into
each hock along the bone and
grill on an electric grill or over
coals (at an adequate distance)
for 1½ hours. • Accompany with
a large salad platter, fresh bread
or pretzels and beer.

Tip: The meat is more flavorful if
cooked over charcoal. One
needs great skill, however, to
judge the heat from the coals
correctly. It should remain con-
stant during the long grilling
time.

## Ham Hocks with Beer

### Easy recipe

Preparation time: 35 minutes
Cooking time: 1½ hours

| |
|---|
| 2 onions |
| ½ cup celery root |
| 3 carrots |
| 2 leeks |
| 2 hind ham hocks, 2 lbs. each, cut with a diamond pattern |
| 1 tsp. each salt and freshly ground black pepper |
| ½ tsp. dried marjoram |
| 3 tbs. bacon fat |
| 2 cups beer |

**P**reheat the oven to 425°. •
Peel and dice the onions,
celery root and carrots. Trim the
leeks, halve lengthwise, wash
and cut in pieces. • Rub the
hocks with the salt, pepper and
marjoram. • Heat the fat in a
roaster and brown the hocks on
all sides 15 minutes. • Add and
briefly sauté the vegetables. Pour
in half the beer and roast the
hocks on the lowest rack of the
oven 1 hour. Baste frequently
with the juices. • After 1 hour
raise the temperature to 475°.
Baste the hocks with the remaining beer and cook an additional
25 minutes. • Keep the hocks
warm in the turned-off oven. •
Deglaze the pan with a little hot
water and puree the liquid with
the vegetables. • Season the
sauce with salt and pepper.
Serve with bread dumplings and
cabbage salad.

# Pepper Tenderloin

## Slightly difficult

Preparation time: 20 minutes
Cooking time: 30 minutes

| |
|---|
| 5 oz. thinly sliced pork fat |
| 1¼ lbs. pork tenderloin |
| ½ tsp. salt |
| 3 tbs. oil |
| 2 tsp. green peppercorns, preserved |
| 4 tbs. coarsely ground herb mustard |
| 1 medium onion |
| 1 medium carrot |
| 2 celery stalks |
| 1 tsp. flour |
| 1 cup beer |
| 1 tsp. caraway |

**P**reheat the oven to 400°. •
Remove any skin and fat
from the meat, then rinse, dry
and rub with salt. • Heat the oil
in a roaster, sear the meat for 3
minutes and let cool. • Crush the
peppercorns and mix with the
mustard. Spread this all over the
meat and then lay it on the pork
fat. Wrap the fat around the tenderloin. • Place the meat in the
roaster and cook on the middle
rack of the oven 20 minutes.
Turn once. • Clean and dice the
vegetables. • Keep the done tenderloin in the turned-off oven. •
Deglaze the pan with a little hot
water and pour the liquid into a
pot. Then steam the vegetables
in the liquid 2 minutes. Sprinkle
the flour over the vegetables and
cook 2 minutes while stirring.
Add the beer and the caraway
and cook 2 more minutes. •
Slice the tenderloin and pour the
sauce over it. • Serve with
steamed spring onions and potatoes.

## Lamb Meat Loaf

### Nutritious

Preparation time: 45 minutes
Cooking time: 30 minutes

¼ cup each coarsely ground green rye, buckwheat and millet

¼ tsp. freshly ground black pepper

1 cup vegetable broth

1 onion

1 tbs. olive oil

¼ cup butter

3 cups savoy cabbage

1¾ lbs. ground lamb

1 egg

1 tsp. sea salt

2 tsp. each freshly chopped thyme and summer savory

2 tbs. buckwheat flour

2 tbs. each tomato paste and crème fraîche

Cook the grains with the pepper for 10 minutes in the vegetable broth. Soak 15 minutes. • Finely chop the onion and sauté until golden in the oil and 1 tablespoon butter. • Blanch the large savoy cabbage leaves 1 minute and cut the ribs flat. • Chop the inside of the cabbage and mix with the ground lamb, egg, salt, herbs and half of the onion. • Mix the remaining onion with the grain. • Arrange the cabbage leaves in a square about 10 to 15 inches wide and spread with the grain mixture. • Shape the meat into a loaf and place in the middle of the cabbage. Wrap the leaves around the meat and bind with string. • Brown the meatloaf in the remaining butter and cook covered in ½ cup water 30 minutes. • Mix the buckwheat flour with the tomato paste, crème fraîche and some water and bind the sauce with it.

## Meat Loaf with Cheese

### Requires some time

Preparation time: 45 minutes
Cooking time: 55 minutes

2 day-old rolls

2 leeks

4 tbs. butter

2 garlic cloves

1¾ lbs. mixed ground meat

3 eggs

1 tbs. pâté spice mix (a mixture of ground white pepper, ginger, bay leaf, mace, allspice and cinnamon)

Salt

Freshly ground black pepper

1 tsp. dried oregano

3 tbs. flour

½ cup milk

½ cup freshly grated Emmenthaler cheese

1 pinch freshly grated nutmeg

Preheat the oven to 475°. • Soak the rolls. • Cut the leeks in fine rings and brown 8 minutes in 2 tablespoons butter. Put the garlic through a garlic press. • Mix the ground meat with the squeezed-out rolls, the eggs, the leeks and the spices. • Grease an ovenproof dish with butter and cook the meat in it for 30 minutes in the oven. • Melt the remaining butter and stir in the flour until golden brown. Stir in the milk and cook 15 minutes. Season the sauce with the cheese, nutmeg, salt and pepper, then pour over the meat-loaf. Cook 25 minutes until golden brown on top.

# Chilled
# Delicacies

## Meatballs with Radish Vinaigrette

### Easy to prepare

Preparation time: 1 hour

| 1 day-old roll |
| 3 green onions |
| 1 small yellow bell pepper |
| 2 tbs. butter |
| 1¼ lbs. mixed ground meat |
| 1 egg |
| 1 egg yolk |
| 1 tsp. each salt and freshly ground white pepper |
| ½ tsp. sweet paprika |
| 1 tsp. Worcestershire sauce |
| 3 tbs. clarified butter |
| 6 tbs. white wine vinegar |
| 8 tbs. oil |
| 2 bunches radishes |
| 1 bunch chives |

Soften the roll in water. • Trim the green onions and cut into thin rings. Prepare the bell pepper and dice. • Sauté the onion 3 minutes in the hot butter, then add the bell pepper and sauté 3 minutes more. • Knead the squeezed-out roll, the vegetables, egg, egg yolk, ½ teaspoon each of salt and pepper, the paprika and Worcestershire sauce into the ground meat. • Shape walnut-sized meatballs from the meat mixture. Sauté in the hot oil, turning, until golden brown. Let the meatballs cool. • Mix the vinegar with the remaining salt and pepper, gradually beat in the oil with a whisk. • Chop the radishes and chives and mix into the sauce. • Serve the meatballs with the vinaigrette and whole-grain rolls.

## Curried Meatballs with Mango Chutney

### Requires some time

Preparation time: 1½ hours
Serves: 8 people

| 1 day-old roll |
| 1 onion |
| 1 pickle |
| ½ cup unsalted peanuts |
| 1 sprig each fresh oregano, rosemary and thyme |
| 2 tbs. bread crumbs |
| 2 eggs |
| 1 tbs. tomato paste |
| 1 tbs. curry powder |
| ½ tsp. each salt and freshly ground black pepper |
| 1¾ lbs. ground beef |
| 8 tbs. oil |
| 1½ lbs. ripe mangos |
| 1 onion |
| 1 garlic clove |

| ¼ cup raisins |
| ½ tsp. each whole allspice and ground mustard |
| 1 tsp. whole coriander |
| 7 tbs. sugar |
| ½ tsp. salt |
| ⅛ tsp. ground ginger |
| ½ cup white wine vinegar |

Soften the roll in water. • Chop the onion, pickle, nuts and herbs. Knead into the ground meat with the bread crumbs, eggs, tomato paste, the squeezed-out roll and the spices. • Shape walnut-sized meatballs and brown until crispy in the oil. Drain and let cool. • Peel the mangos, onion and garlic; finely chop. • Rinse the raisins in hot water and grind with the spices in a mortar. Mix with the mangos, onion, garlic and vinegar. Stir 20 minutes over low heat until thick and let cool. • Serve

the chutney with the meatballs. • The chutney can be refrigerated in a tightly closed jar up to 3 months.

## Steak Tartare on Watercress with Quail Eggs

**Nutritious, quick**

Preparation time: 20 minutes

| |
|---|
| 2 bunches watercress |
| 14 oz. steak tartare |
| ½ tsp. freshly ground black pepper |
| 1 bunch radishes |
| 8 hard-boiled quail eggs |
| 2 tbs. whole-grain sesame seeds |
| Sea salt in a mill |

Cut the cress from the bed, rinse and drain well in a sieve. Arrange on four salad plates. • Shape four equal patties from the tartare and place on the cress. Sprinkle each portion with some pepper. • Wash the radishes, dry, trim and halve. • Peel and halve the quail eggs lengthwise. Garnish each plate with radishes and egg halves. • Roast the sesame seeds in an oil-free pan. Turn the seeds until they begin to pop and have a nice aroma. • Sprinkle the seeds over the meat. • Serve with the salt in a mill or in a salt shaker.

Tip: Because ground meats spoil very rapidly, buy steak for tartare from the butcher and have him grind it on the day it is to be used.

## Seasoned Steak Tartare

**Quick, slightly expensive**

Preparation time: 30 minutes

| |
|---|
| 1 large white onion |
| 4 small pickles |
| ¼ cup olives, stuffed with pimentos |
| 1 tbs. small capers |
| 1 tsp. spicy mustard |
| 1 tsp. salt |
| ½ tsp. each freshly ground black pepper and hot paprika |
| 2 egg yolks |
| 14 oz. steak tartare |
| ½ bunch watercress |
| 2 tomatoes |

Peel the onion and cut several very thin rings from the middle. Finely chop the remaining onion. • Chop 1 pickle into a fan shape; finely chop the others. • Halve 4 olives; chop the others with the capers. • Mix all the chopped ingredients into the tartare with the mustard, salt, pepper, paprika and egg yolks. • Arrange the tartare on a platter and garnish with the prepared pickle, the onion rings and the olives. • Cut the watercress from the bed, rinse and drain. • Wash and dry the tomatoes, cut into eighths and arrange with the cress around the tartare. • Good with whole-grain bread or a fresh baguette and butter.

## Pickled Beef Tongue with Sprouts

### Nutritious, slightly difficult

Sprouting time: 5 days
Cooking time: 2½ hours
Finishing time: 45 minutes
Cooling time: 3 hours
Serves: 6 people

| |
|---|
| 1 tbs. each germinated mustard, radish, watercress and mung bean seeds |
| 1¾ lbs. lightly pickled beef tongue |
| 1 onion |
| ½ bunch soup herbs |
| 1 bay leaf |
| 5 each juniper berries and black peppercorns |
| 1 cup dry red wine |
| 4 tbs. red wine vinegar |
| 3 tbs. soy sauce |
| 1 tbs. apple juice concentrate |
| 2 tbs. unflavored gelatin |
| 1 tbs. oil |
| 1 cup sour cream |
| 2 tbs. safflower seed oil |
| 1 tbs. each mildly spicy mustard and honey |
| 2 tbs. chopped chives |
| ⅛ tsp. freshly ground black pepper |

At least 5 days prior to preparing the tongue, sprout the seeds separately in a sprouting container. • Spread the mustard, radish and cress seeds on a flat plate covered with a layer of cellulose. Soak the cellulose with water, press the seeds slightly and spray them in the mornings and evenings so that they remain damp. • Pour the mung beans in a jam jar and let stand covered with water for 5 days. Cover the jar with coarse cloth and pour the water out through the cloth. Replace the water twice a day and pour off immediately. • Keep all the seeds in a bright, warm place. • After about 5 days let the sprouts drain. • Wash the tongue thoroughly and brush the upper side well. • Peel and quarter the onion. Wash, trim and coarsely chop the soup herbs. • Bring about 2 quarts of water with the prepared vegetables, the bay leaf, the juniper berries and the peppercorns to a boil. Let the tongue cook in the water over low heat 2½ hours. • Rinse the tongue under cold water and remove the skin. Cut the tongue in slices about 1 inch thick and arrange in a fan shape on a platter. • Strain 1 cup of the cooking liquid and heat, but do not boil, with the wine, 2 tablespoons of vinegar, 1 tablespoon of soy sauce and the apple juice concentrate. • Dissolve the gelatin in the hot broth, then allow to cool until it begins to gel. Pour the gelatin mixture over the slices of tongue and cool until firm (2 to 3 hours) in the refrigerator. • Arrange the mustard, radish and cress sprouts on the tongue. • Sauté the mung bean sprouts for 3 minutes in the oil and mix with 1 tablespoon soy sauce. Arrange on the tongue. • Blend the sour cream with the safflower seed oil, the remaining vinegar and soy sauce, the mustard, honey, chives and pepper. Serve as a sauce with the tongue.

## Ham and Roast in Aspic

### Requires some time

Preparation time: 1 hour
Cooling time: 4 to 5 hours
Serves: 6 people

| 1 cup beef broth |
| 1 bunch soup herbs |
| 1 onion |
| 1 bay leaf |
| 2 cloves |
| 1 sprig fresh rosemary |
| 1 cup dry white wine |
| ¼ tsp. each salt and freshly ground white pepper |
| ½ tsp. sugar |
| 2 tbs. cognac |
| 3 tbs. unflavored gelatin |
| 2 lean cooked ham |
| 1 bunch parsley |

**B**ring the beef broth to a boil. Gently simmer the trimmed, chopped soup herbs, the quartered onion and the spices in the broth 15 minutes. • Strain the broth and season with the wine, salt, pepper, sugar and cognac. • Dissolve the gelatin in the hot broth. Place to the side. • Remove the fat rind from the ham and cut into 1-inch cubes. • Rinse and chop the parsley. • Mix the ham cubes and parsley in a rectangular pan with the gelling broth. Cover and place in the refrigerator until firm (about 4 to 5 hours). • Turn the aspic out of the mold onto a platter and cut into slices. • Serve with bread and radish salad.

## Pork Roast in Aspic

### Requires some time

Preparation time: 1 hour
Cooling time: 3 hours

| 2 carrots |
| 1 qt. beef broth |
| 4 tbs. unflavored gelatin |
| 1¼ lbs. cold pork roast, boned |
| 2 hard-boiled eggs |
| ¾ cup mixed pickles |
| ½ bunch parsley |
| 2 tbs. white wine vinegar |
| ½ tsp. each salt and freshly ground black pepper |

**R**inse, peel and slice the carrots (use a decorating knife if desired) and cook in 1 cup broth. • Cut the roast in very thin slices. • Peel and slice the eggs. Chop the mixed pickles.

Wash the parsley and pick the leaves from the stems. • Drain the carrots and heat the liquid with the remaining beef broth. • Dissolve the gelatin in the hot broth and vinegar. • Pour a thin layer of gelatin into a dish and place in the refrigerator until firm. • Arrange a portion of the vegetables and egg slices on the firm gelatin, cover with another layer of gelatin and chill. • Add the meat slices in small portions to the dish, together with the remaining vegetables and egg slices. Salt and pepper each layer before covering with gelatin and letting each layer chill until firm. • Place the aspic in the refrigerator for an additional 3 hours or until completely firm.

# Cold Meat Loaf with Rye

### Nutritious, requires some time

Preparation time: 1 hour
Cooking time: 1 hour
Cooling time: 3 hours
Serves: 6 people

| |
|---|
| 4 slices smoked bacon |
| 4 tbs. oil |
| 1 cup onions |
| 3 garlic cloves |
| 3 tbs. each crushed green rye and rye |
| 1 tbs. each granulated bouillon and mustard seeds |
| 1 tsp. each freshly ground black pepper, ground coriander, powdered ginger and dried thyme |
| 1 pinch freshly ground nutmeg |
| ½ tsp. salt |
| 1 lb. ground beef |
| Butter for the dish |

Cut the bacon into small cubes, fry in 2 tablespoons oil and set to the side. • Peel and chop the onions and garlic, sauté until golden in the remaining oil, mix with the bacon and crushed grains and sauté for an additional 5 minutes. Pour in 1 cup water, add all the spices and simmer gently 5 minutes. Let soak 15 minutes with no heat. • Preheat the oven to 400°. • Knead the grain mixture into the meat and fill a buttered loaf pan (about 10 inches long). Bake 1 hour on the middle rack of the oven. • Cool the meat 10 minutes in the pan and then wrap in aluminum foil. Cool in the refrigerator 3 hours. • Cut the meat into slices and serve with herbed crème fraîche.

## Ground Meat Terrine

### Requires some time

Preparation time: 40 minutes
Cooking time: 50 minutes
Cooling time: 2 hours
Serves: 6 people

| |
|---|
| 3 garlic cloves |
| 1 large onion |
| 2 tbs. butter |
| ½ cup instant rice |
| 1½ lbs. mixed ground meats |
| 1 tbs. tomato paste |
| 4 eggs |
| ¾ cup crème fraîche |
| 1½ tsp. each salt and freshly ground black pepper |
| 2 tsp. pâté spice mix (a mixture of ground white pepper, ginger, bay leaf, mace, allspice and cinnamon) |
| 1 tsp. sweet paprika |
| 1¼ cups hulled peas |
| 5 tbs. red wine vinegar |
| 7 tbs. oil |
| 1 bunch basil |
| 2 bunches chives |
| 1 bunch parsley |
| Butter for the dish |

Chop the garlic and onion and sauté until translucent in the butter. • Cook the rice. • Knead the above ingredients into the meat with the tomato paste, the eggs, the crème fraîche, 1 teaspoon each salt and pepper, and the remaining spices. • Preheat the oven to 350°. • Mix the peas into the meat and fill the mixture into a buttered loaf pan. Bake on the middle rack of the oven 50 minutes. • Cool the terrine in the refrigerator 2 hours. • Blend the vinegar with the remaining salt and pepper, the oil and the chopped herbs. Serve with the terrine.

## Vegetable Meat Squares

### Easy to prepare

Preparation time: 40 minutes
Cooking time: 50 minutes
Serves: 8 people

| |
|---|
| 2 day-old rolls |
| 1½ cups cucumber |
| 3 large white onions |
| 1 garlic clove |
| 1 cup tomatoes |
| 2 lbs. ground beef |
| 3 tbs. flour |
| 5 eggs |
| 5 tbs. tomato paste |
| 1 tsp. salt |
| ½ tsp. cayenne pepper |
| 1 cup sour cream |
| ½ cup cream |
| ½ tsp. each freshly ground black pepper and dried oregano |

Soften the rolls. • Cut the cucumbers in slices. • Dice 2 onions and slice 1 in thin rings. Chop the garlic. • Cut the tomatoes into slices. • Knead the ground meat with the squeezed-out rolls, the diced onion, the garlic, the flour, 3 eggs, the tomato paste and the salt and cayenne pepper. • Preheat the oven to 400°. • Spread the meat mixture on a baking sheet and arrange the vegetables on top. Bake on the middle rack of the oven 30 minutes. • Blend the remaining eggs with the sour cream, cream, pepper and oregano. Pour over the vegetables and let thicken. • Cool and cut into squares.

## Roast Beef with Horseradish Sauce

**Slightly expensive**

Preparation time: 25 minutes
Cooking time: 45 minutes
Cooling time: 1 hour
Serves: 6 people

2 lbs. roast beef

3 tbs. oil

½ tsp. each freshly ground black pepper and dried rosemary

1 tsp. each mustard and salt

1 large, tart apple

1 cup cream

1 pinch sugar

⅛ tsp. salt

½ tsp. freshly ground white pepper

2 tbs. freshly ground horseradish

Cut a crosshatch pattern into the fat layer of the roast beef. • Blend the oil with the pepper, rosemary and mustard; rub the meat with the mixture and marinate 20 minutes. • Preheat the oven to 425°. • Rinse out a flat roasting pan. Sprinkle the salt on the meat and with the fat side up place on the pan on the middle rack of the oven. Bake the meat 25 minutes. • Reduce the temperature to 325° and bake the roast beef an additional 20 minutes. • Peel the apple, quarter and grate. • Beat the cream until stiff with the sugar, salt and pepper. Fold in the grated apple and horse-radish. • Let the roast beef stand in the turned-off oven. • Slice the roast beef thinly and serve with the horseradish sauce. • Serve with bread.

## Roast Beef with Mustard Sauce

**Slightly expensive**

Preparation time: 40 minutes
Cooking time: 30 minutes
Cooling time: 1 hour
Serves: 6 people

2 lbs. roast beef

1 tsp. salt

1 tsp. freshly ground black pepper

4 garlic cloves

6 tbs. olive oil

3 egg yolks

3 tbs. spicy mustard

1 tsp. balsamic vinegar

⅛ tsp. cayenne pepper

4 green onions

Preheat the oven to 475°. • Rinse the meat, dry and rub with salt and pepper. • Peel the garlic cloves and crush with a garlic press. Mix with 2 table-spoons olive oil and rub onto the meat. Bake the meat on a bak-ing sheet lined with aluminum foil on the middle rack of the oven for 30 minutes. After 15 minutes reduce the heat to 400°. • Let the meat stand 20 minutes in the turned-off oven. • Wrap the roast beef in the aluminum foil and chill. • Blend the remain-ing oil with the egg yolks and the mustard; season with the salt and pepper, the vinegar and cayenne pepper. • Cut the green onions in thin rings and mix into the sauce. • Slice the cold roast beef thinly and pour the sauce over it.

## Saddle of Hare with Apricots

**Slightly difficult, slightly expensive**

Preparation time: 30 minutes
Cooking time: 30 minutes
Cooling time: 1 hour
Finishing time: 30 minutes

1¾ lbs. saddle of hare

1 tsp. salt

¼ tsp. freshly ground white pepper

1 tsp. dried thyme

3 slices bacon

7 oz. chicken livers

1 medium onion

1 cup mushrooms

½ cup Madeira wine

1 tsp. pâté spice mix (a mixture of ground white pepper, ginger, bay leaf, mace, allspice and cinnamon)

5 tbs. butter

⅔ cup purple grapes

1 cup canned apricots

Preheat the oven to 400°. • Rinse the hare under cold water, dry and remove any skin. • Rub the meat with half of the salt, the pepper and half of the thyme. • Chop the bacon. Rinse the chicken livers, dab dry and remove any skin or fat. • Fry the bacon and brown the hare well on all sides in the pan. • Put the hare and the bacon fat in a roaster and bake 30 minutes on the second lowest rack of the oven. • After 20 minutes place the chicken livers around the hare. • Peel and finely chop the onion. Wash and dry the mushrooms, then trim and chop. • After 30 minutes baking time, remove the hare and chicken livers from the roaster and let cool. • Sauté the mushrooms and onions in the roaster on top of

the range. Pour in the Madeira wine and let thicken while stirring. Season the mixture with the remaining salt and pepper, the pâté spice mix and the remaining thyme. • Finely chop the livers and mix into the cooled mushroom-onion mixture. Cream the butter and blend into the mixture. • Remove both filets from the saddle of hare and cut on the diagonal into slices. Spread a little of the liver cream on each slice and reposition against the bone. • Put the remainder of the liver cream in a pastry bag and squirt a decorative garland on the mid-line of the saddle of hare. • Wash and drain the grapes, then halve and remove the seeds. • Drain the apricot halves and place on the garland with the pitted side up. Place a grape half on each apricot. Fill the remaining apricot halves with liver cream and garnish with a

grape, then arrange around the saddle of hare. • Serve with Cumberland sauce and Waldorf salad.

Tip: If desired use calf liver for the liver cream instead of chicken livers.

## Pork Tenderloin with Lemon Mayonnaise

### Easy to prepare

Preparation time: 30 minutes
Cooking time: 30 minutes

| |
|---|
| 1¼ lbs. pork tenderloin |
| 3 tbs. clarified butter |
| 1 tsp. each salt and freshly ground white pepper |
| 2 egg yolks |
| 1 cup soybean oil |
| Juice and grated rind of 1 lemon |
| 1 bunch lemon balm |

Rinse the tenderloin under cold water, dab dry and remove any fat and skin. Sear well on all sides in the hot clarified butter. • Cook the tenderloin covered over low heat 30 minutes. Salt and pepper, wrap in aluminum foil and let cool. • Beat the egg yolks for the lemon mayonnaise with the salt and pepper in a bowl. Add the oil in a fine stream while beating with a whisk. Beat until all ingredients are combined and the mixture holds peaks. • Season the mayonnaise with the lemon juice and rind. • Rinse the lemon balm and pick the leaves from the stems. Cut into small strips and blend into the mayonnaise shortly before serving. • Cut the tenderloin into slices about ¼ inch thick and arrange on a platter. Serve with the mayonnaise. • Good with oven-fresh bread.

## Pork Tenderloin in Ham

### Slightly difficult

Preparation time: 30 minutes
Cooking time: 45 minutes
Serves: 6 people

| |
|---|
| 1¾ lbs. pork tenderloin |
| ½ tsp. each salt, freshly ground black pepper and sweet paprika |
| 1 tsp. spicy mustard |
| 8 oz. thinly sliced smoked ham |
| 3 tbs. bacon fat |
| 1 cup beef broth |

Rinse the tenderloin, dry and remove any skin and fat. Rub with the salt, pepper, paprika and mustard. • Preheat the oven to 350°. • Arrange half of the ham slices on a work surface so that they overlap slightly. Place the meat on the ham and cover with the remaining ham slices. Tie with kitchen string. • Heat the bacon fat in a roaster and sear the meat on all sides. Pour in the beef broth and bake the tenderloin 45 minutes on the middle rack of the oven. • Cut the cold roast into slices.

Tip: Use salt sparingly, as the smoked ham also adds salt to the roast.

## Beef Brisket with Vegetable Sauce

### Requires some time

Preparation time: 45 minutes
Cooking time: 2 to 3 hours
Serves: 6 people

| |
| --- |
| 2 onions |
| 2 carrots |
| 4 garlic cloves |
| 3 thin leeks |
| 3 stalks celery |
| 2 lbs. beef brisket |
| 1 bay leaf |
| 1 tsp. each dried thyme, rosemary, oregano, salt and freshly ground black pepper |
| Juice of 1 lemon |
| 1 tbs. balsamic vinegar |
| 1 bunch basil |

**P**eel the onions, carrots and garlic. Trim and rinse the leeks and celery. Cut all the vegetables in pieces. • Rinse the meat. Place the meat, vegetables and spices in a pot and barely cover with water. Bring to a boil. • Skim any foam that collects, then cook covered over low heat 2 hours. • Puree the vegetables with a little broth: use the remainder of the broth for another dish. • Season the vegetable sauce with the lemon juice, vinegar, salt and pepper. • Rinse the basil, pick the leaves and sprinkle over the sauce. • Cut the meat in slices and pour the sauce over it.

## Beef Brisket with Cucumber Sauce

### Requires some time

Preparation time: 40 minutes
Cooking time: 2½ hours
Serves: 6 people

| |
| --- |
| 2 lbs. beef brisket |
| 1 bay leaf |
| 1 tsp. salt |
| 1 tsp. black peppercorns |
| 1 onion |
| 2 leeks |
| 1 carrot |
| ½ cup celery root |
| 1 salad cucumber |
| 1 cup cottage cheese or ricotta |
| 1 cup buttermilk |
| 3 green onions |
| 2 tbs. oil |
| 2 tbs. white wine vinegar |
| 1 pinch freshly ground black pepper |

**P**lace the meat with the bay leaf, half the salt and the peppercorns in a pot. • Peel and rinse the onion, leeks, carrot and celery root. Cut into pieces, add to the meat and barely cover with water. Bring to a boil and skim any foam that collects. • Cover and cook over low heat 2½ hours. • Let the meat cool. Use the broth for another purpose. • Peel the cucumber and halve lengthwise. Remove the seeds and cut into pieces. Puree with the fresh cheese and buttermilk. • Trim and rinse the green onions, then cut into thin rings. Mix into the cucumber sauce with the oil and vinegar. Season the sauce with the remaining salt and pepper. • Slice the meat and serve with the sauce.

## Mixed Meat Platter with Green Sauce

**Requires some time, slightly expensive**

Preparation time: 1 hour
Cooking time: 2½ hours
Cooling time: 1 hour
Serves: 8 people

For the meat platter:

| |
|---|
| 2 leeks |
| 1 cup celery root |
| 2 carrots |
| 1 large onion |
| 2 lbs. beef shank, boned |
| 1½ lbs. veal tongue |
| 1 bay leaf |
| ½ tsp. black peppercorns |
| 1 tbs. salt |
| 1¾ lbs. chicken breast, with skin and bones |

For the sauce:

| |
|---|
| 2 onions |
| 2 garlic cloves |
| 4 anchovies |
| 2 tbs. capers |
| 2 bunches parsley |
| 1 lemon |
| 2 tbs. bread crumbs |
| ½ cup olive oil |
| ⅛ tsp. each salt, freshly ground white pepper and sugar |

Trim the leeks, cut open lengthwise, rinse and either halve or quarter, depending on size. Peel, rinse and coarsely chop the celery root and carrots. Peel and halve the onion. • Rinse the beef and veal tongue. Scrub the top of the veal tongue. • Bring 2 quarts of water to a boil. Add the meat, the tongue, the vegetables, the bay leaf, peppercorns and salt. Let boil, skimming any foam that collects. • Cover the meat and cook over low heat 2½ hours. • Rinse the chicken breasts and add to the meat after 2 hours, so that they cook together 30 minutes. • Peel the onions and garlic for the sauce. Finely chop the onions and put the garlic through a press. • Rinse the anchovies and dab dry. Chop finely with the capers. • Rinse the parsley, spin dry and chop. • Rinse the lemon under warm water, dry and finely grate the rind. Squeeze the juice. • Mix the onions, garlic, anchovies, capers, parsley, lemon rind and bread crumbs. Gradually blend in the lemon juice and oil, then season the sauce with the salt, pepper and sugar. Cover and refrigerate so that the flavors blend. • Remove the meat from the broth. Skin the tongue and remove any tendons or gristle. Skin and bone the chicken. Cover the meat with broth and chill in the refrigerator. • Carve the meat and arrange on a large platter. Serve with the sauce. • Good accompanied with a mixed salad, hard-boiled eggs and fresh bread.

## Veal Salad

### Nutritious

Soaking time: 12 hours
Preparation time: 1 hour

| | |
|---|---|
| 2¼ cups spelt (German wheat) | |
| 1 tsp. finely chopped basil | |
| 1½ tsp. sea salt | |
| 1 lb. veal neck | |
| 1 onion | |
| 1 lb. zucchini | |
| 3 tbs. safflower seed oil | |
| ⅛ tsp. freshly ground white pepper | |
| ⅔ cup hulled peas | |
| 1 tbs. chopped chives | |
| 1 tsp. fresh sage, chopped | |
| 4 tbs. cream | |
| 2 tbs. lemon juice | |

**B**ring the spelt to a boil in 2 cups of water and soak covered 12 hours. • Bring to a second boil with the basil and 1 teaspoon salt. Add the meat and some water if needed. Cook everything until tender, about 45 minutes. • Pour the meat and spelt into a large sieve and reserve the broth. • Cut the onion into rings and julienne the zucchini. • Sauté the onion in the hot oil until translucent, add the zucchini and salt and pepper. Sauté over low heat 2 minutes. • Add the peas and the broth. Let most of the liquid cook off. • Julienne the meat and mix with the spelt, the vegetables, the herbs, cream and lemon juice. Cover and marinate in the refrigerator.

## Beef Salad

### Requires some time

Preparation time: 1½ hours
Marinating time: 1 hour
Serves: 8 people

| | |
|---|---|
| 2 onions | |
| 1 bay leaf | |
| 2 cloves | |
| 1 bunch soup herbs | |
| 2 tsp. salt | |
| 2 lbs. beef shoulder | |
| 1 each yellow, green and red bell peppers | |
| 1 pickle | |
| 2 tbs. soy sauce | |
| 3 tbs. red wine vinegar | |
| 1 tsp. freshly ground black pepper | |
| 1 pinch sugar | |
| 1 tsp. mustard | |
| ½ tsp. sweet paprika | |
| 2 tbs. chopped chives | |

**P**eel 1 onion and stud with the bay leaf and cloves. Bring 1 quart of water to a boil with the onion, the prepared soup herbs and 1 teaspoon salt. • Add and cook the meat over low heat 1½ hours. • Skim any foam that collects. Cover the pot, but leave a partial opening. • Rinse and trim the bell peppers, then cut into strips. • Cut the remaining onion into rings and the pickle into slices. • Blend the soy sauce with the vinegar, the remaining salt and the spices. • Chill the meat in the broth. Remove any fat and julienne the meat. Mix with the vegetables and sauce. • Marinate the salad 1 hour and sprinkle with the chives.

# Liver Terrine with Grapes

### Famous recipe, slightly difficult

Preparation time: 40 minutes
Cooking time: 50 minutes
Finishing time: 40 minutes

| | |
|---|---|
| A 10-inch spring form pan | |
| 14 oz. chicken livers | |
| 4 slices bacon | |
| 2 medium onions | |
| 3 slices toast | |
| ½ tsp. salt | |
| ¼ tsp. freshly ground white pepper | |
| 3 tsp. pâté spice (a mixture of ground white pepper, ginger, bay leaf, mace, allspice and cinnamon) | |
| 4 tbs. medium-dry sherry | |
| 1¼ lbs. veal sausage | |
| 1 tbs. unflavored gelatin | |
| ½ cup each white and red grapes | |
| 1 cup Cumberland sauce | |
| 1 cup cream | |
| 2 tbs. cream thickener, if desired | |
| 1 tsp. sugar | |
| 1 pinch salt | |
| 1 tbs. freshly grated horseradish | |
| Butter for the pan | |

**R**inse the chicken livers, dab dry and remove any skin or fat. • Cube the bacon. Chop the onions. • Soften the toast in cold water. • Preheat the oven to 350°. Grease the spring form with butter. • Fry the bacon, then brown the chicken livers 3 minutes while turning. Add the onion and sauté until translucent. • Mix the spices and sherry into the livers, remove from the heat and cool. • Mix the sausage with the squeezed-out toast. • Coarsely chop the chicken livers and mix them with the onions and bacon into the sausage. • Fill the spring form with the meat mixture and bake on the second lowest rack of the oven 50 minutes. • Let the terrine rest in the pan 10 minutes and then cool on a platter. • Rinse, dry, halve and remove the seeds from the grapes. Place the grapes with the round side up on the terrine, leaving about a 1½-inch border uncovered. • Heat the Cumberland sauce. Dissolve the gelatin in the warm sauce and set aside. • Beat the cream with the sugar and salt. Fold in the horseradish. • Spread the horseradish cream on the sides of the terrine. Fill a pastry bag with the remaining cream and decorate the border of the terrine with a garland. • Pour the gelling Cumberland sauce over the grapes. Cool in the refrigerator until firm and ready to serve. • Serve with fresh bread and a salad.

Tip: Substitute calf or beef liver for chicken liver.

## Wild Pig Terrine

### Slightly expensive

Preparation time: 1 hour
Cooking time: 1½ hours
Serves: 8 people

| |
|---|
| 1 cup mushrooms |
| 2 lbs. wild pig, boned |
| ¾ cup white onions |
| 1 bunch parsley |
| 8 slices fat bacon |
| 9 oz. chicken livers |
| ¼ cup butter |
| ½ tsp. each salt and freshly ground black pepper |
| 1 tsp. dried rosemary |
| 4 tbs. Madeira wine |

Clean the mushrooms. • Remove any tendons and skin from the meat, rinse, dry and cube. • Cut the onions into eighths. Rinse the parsley and spin dry. Reserve 1 sprig and chop the remainder. Cube the bacon. • Remove skin and fat from the livers, rinse, dab dry and brown in the butter 5 minutes. • Grind the meat with the onions and bacon twice with the finest blade of a meat grinder. • Cube the livers and mix into the ground meat with the butter from browning, the chopped parsley, the spices and the wine. • Preheat the oven to 400°. • Put half the meat mixture into an ovenproof dish, cover with the mushrooms and the remaining meat mixture. Cover the dish with a lid. • Bake the dish in a pan of hot water on the middle rack of the oven 1½ hours. • Cool the terrine in the refrigerator. Garnish with the remaining parsley. Serve with cranberry jelly and fresh white bread.

## Savory Veal Terrine

**Requires some time, slightly difficult**

Preparation time: 1½ hours
Cooling time: 12 hours
Cooking time: 50 minutes

For a 5 cup crockery baking dish with lid

| |
|---|
| 14 oz. veal tenderloin |
| 9 oz. pork tenderloin |
| 1½ lbs. fat unsmoked bacon, thinly sliced |
| 1½ tsp. salt |
| ½ tsp. each green pepper, basil, sage and thyme, all dried |
| 4 slices white bread without crust |
| 1 egg white |
| 1 cup cream |
| 2 shallots |
| 7 oz. calf liver |
| ¼ cup butter |
| 2 tbs. each cognac and Cointreau |
| 1 garlic clove |
| ⅛ tsp. each powdered ginger and powdered cardamom |
| ¾ cup mushrooms |
| ¼ lb. cooked ham with no fat |
| 2 tbs. chopped parsley |

**R**inse the meat, dry and remove any tendons, skin or fat. • Cut the meat in thin slices and arrange on a platter with about ½ pound bacon slices. • Mix 1 teaspoon salt with the remaining spices and sprinkle over the meat. • Slice the bread in thin slices and lay on the meat. • Beat the egg white with 6 tablespoons cream and trickle over the meat. • Cover the platter and refrigerate 12 hours. • Peel and chop the shallots. Wash, skin and cube the calf liver. • Melt 2 tablespoons butter and sauté the shallots until yellow. Add the liver and brown 2 minutes, then remove from the heat. • Grind the meat with the bacon and bread twice with the finest blade of a meat grinder. Knead the farce with the cognac, Cointreau, the remaining salt, the pressed garlic clove, the ginger and the cardamom. Place in the refrigerator. • Clean the mushrooms and slice. Cut the ham into small cubes. • Preheat the oven to 425°. • Line the crockery loaf pan completely with part of the remaining bacon slices. The bacon should extend beyond the rim of the pan. • Mix the farce over ice with the remaining cream and the parsley until it glistens. Mix in the shallots, the calf liver, the mushrooms and the ham. Fill the terrine and fold the bacon over the sides, then cover the top with the remaining bacon slices. Place the lid on top and set the terrine in a pan filled with hot water. Bake on the lowest rack of the oven 50 minutes; reduce the temperature to 350°. • Cool the terrine after baking and remove the bacon slices from the top before serving. • Good with a mixed salad and bread.

## Lamb Pâté en Croûte with Sweetbreads

**Slightly expensive, slightly difficult**

Preparation time: 1½ hours
Cooling time: 12 hours
Cooking time: 1 hour

For a 10-inch spring form pan

1 lb. lamb shoulder, boned

4 slices white bread without crusts

1 pinch each dried peppermint, dried rosemary and freshly ground white pepper

½ tsp. salt

1 egg white

1 cup cream

14 oz. lamb sweetbreads (if unavailable, use veal sweetbreads)

3 tbs. canned truffles

3 tsp. fresh basil, chopped

2¼ cups flour

¾ cup butter

1 egg

1 egg yolk

**R**inse the lamb, dry and re-move any tendons or skin. Cut into thin strips and arrange on a platter. • Cut the bread in strips and lay on the meat. • Mix the spices with 1 pinch of salt and sprinkle over the bread. • Beat the egg white with 6 table-spoons cream and trickle over the bread. Cover the platter and refrigerate 12 hours. • Soak the sweetbreads, changing the water frequently. • Simmer the sweet-breads gently in salt water for 10 minutes. Cool in fresh water and remove all skin and any bloody parts or gristle. Cube and place to the side. • Beat the remaining cream until stiff. • Grind the meat with the bread twice through the finest blade of a meat grinder. Mix the meat with the cream over ice cubes. • Chop the truffles and mix with the truffle juice, the basil and the sweetbreads into the farce. Place in the refrigerator. • Preheat the oven to 425°. • Prepare a dough from the flour, butter, one egg, the remaining salt and 1 table-spoon ice cold water. Roll out 2 crusts of about 12 inches in di-ameter. Line the spring form with 1 crust. Pierce several times with a fork. • Fill the pan with the farce and place the second crust on top. Trim the edges and press them together. • Pierce the upper crust with a fork several times so that steam can escape during the baking. • Cut small decorative pieces from the re-maining dough. • Beat the egg yolk and brush the surface crust with it. Place the decorative crusts on the pastry and brush with egg yolk. • Bake 1 hour on the middle rack of the oven. If necessary during the baking time, cover the upper crust with parchment paper so that it does not brown too much. • Cool the pâté 15 minutes in the pan, then finish cooling on a kitchen rack.

# Index